T0151044

Waterfalls

of **MINNESOTA'S NORTH SHORE** & *More*

A Guide for Sightseers,
Hikers & Romantics
Expanded Second Edition

Eve & Gary Wallinga

North Shore Press
Grand Marais, Minnesota

Maps and photos by Gary Wallinga

Cover photo of Cascade River by Paul Sundberg

Graphic Design by Katie Viren,
Kyle Sobanja and Amber Pratt

North Shore Press
A division of Northern Wilds Media, Inc.
1708 W. Hwy 61, P.O. Box 26
Grand Marais, MN 55604
(218) 387-9475

www.northernwilds.com

Copyright 2006, 2015 by Eve and Gary Wallinga

All rights reserved. No part of this publication may
be reproduced, stored in a retrieval system, or
transmitted, in any form or by any means, electronic,
mechanical, photocopying, recording, or otherwise,
without the prior written permission of the publisher.

ISBN: 978-0-9740207-6-1

Printed in Canada by Friesens

10 9 8 7 6 5

To our amazing children, Nissa and Dane.

He kept his eyes upon the waterfall.
The clear stream, like a luminous column
amongst the moss and the stones, held its noble outline
unaltered through all the hours of the day and night.
In the midst of it there was a small projecting cascade,
where the tumbling water struck a rock. That, too,
stood out immutable, like a fresh crack in the marble
of the cataract. If he returned in ten years, he would
find it unchanged, in the same form, like a
harmonious and immortal work of art.
Still it was, each second, new particles of water hurled
over the edge, rushing into a precipice and disappearing.
It was a flight, a whirl, an incessant catastrophe.

—Isak Dinesen from *Winter's Tales*

Acknowledgments

Thank you to everyone who helped with this book, directly and indirectly.

Thanks to those folks at the Minnesota Department of Natural Resources, who provided information throughout our work on this book.

Thank you specifically to Ronald VanBergen of the Finland Area Fisheries, Vernon Imgrund of the Grand Marais Area Fisheries, and Daniel Dexter of the Duluth Area Fisheries for the hours you so patiently spent with us. Also, a special thanks to Michael Lee, DNR botanist/ecologist for the Minnesota County Biological Survey, for your help with the aerial photos, maps, and so many other things.

Thank you to Shawn Perich, our editor and publisher, who responded enthusiastically to our book query, who believed in this project, and who was uniquely qualified to make this book a reality. We are honored to have had the opportunity to work with you.

Thanks to the members of Eve's writers group, for your word-crafting skills, encouragement, and support—Julie Evans, Judy Kallestad, Linda Marie, and Tom Mitzel.

Thanks to our wonderful friends, Tom Olson and Merle Sykora, for introducing us to the beauty of the North Shore years ago, and for allowing us to enjoy your unending hospitality at your beautiful home on "The Shore."

We are indebted to Toni Murphy and Sigurd Hoppe for helping us to become better partners in writing and in life.

Thanks to Edward Weir. You provided inspiration and impetus for this project. As you once said to Eve, and she now says to you—I greatly doubt that the book would have happened without you.

And thank you to Dr. Frank DellaCroce and the staff of the Center for Restorative Breast Surgery, New Orleans, for helping to restore my body and spirit in time for the expanded edition of the book.

Contents

2 Minnesota Waterfalls and Map of Rivers

Introduction

In 1983, my husband and I settled in Seattle, Washington, where he began his internship training in clinical psychology and I became a new mother. It was a month before the clouds cleared enough to reveal that we had an ethereal view of Mount Rainier from our apartment. For flat-landers from the Midwest, this was quite exciting. The mountains of the Cascades and the Olympic Peninsula beckoned, but traveling several hours in the car with a very vocal new baby proved difficult.

One day, while perusing a bookstore in the local mall, we discovered a book, *Waterfalls of the Pacific Northwest*. The cover photo featured twin cascades free-falling a hundred feet into an exotic fern and moss-covered grotto. We wanted to be there! We purchased the book, and despite the baby's protests in the car, set off to explore the waterfalls described in the guide.

Our quest for falls soon became a passion. Eager with anticipation while hiking the trails, our ears strained to hear the rumble of the falls ahead. When we came within earshot, it was difficult not to sprint ahead of the one with the baby in tow. The first to glimpse the white water through the trees exclaimed, "There it is! I see the falls!" And our steps quickened. We never knew what we would find. Each waterfall was unique and never disappointing. The book introduced us to what became a lifetime love—waterfalls. And, we thought, what fun it would be, to someday write a book like that!

Twenty years later and half a continent away, we decided to make that dream a reality. Moving to Minnesota, we found to our delight that Lake Superior's North Shore is a treasure trove of fabulous falls. Many are well-known to folks who live nearby or visit "The Shore." But we discovered many lesser-known gems. We were surprised to find that no one had produced a guide to these falls, despite the plethora of books regarding various aspects of Lake Superior.

After studying numerous waterfall guides from other parts of the country for user-friendly formats, and compiling North Shore waterfall information from other publications, we began our work. We talked with local residents, park staff, and Department of Natural Resources personnel, some whose job it was to literally walk the rivers and streams from Lake Superior to their sources. Thus *Waterfalls of Minnesota's North Shore: A Guide for Sightseers, Hikers and Romantics* was born.

It's been eight years since that first edition cascaded off the press. Little did we know the book would become a best-seller, requiring several printing runs. The best part of the experience, though, has been the positive feedback we've received from so many people.

Particularly memorable was a young couple we met at a book signing at The Trading Post in Grand Marias. They brought their well-thumbed copy, stuck throughout with different colored post-it notes marking the waterfalls they'd visited and had yet to visit. We've received thanks for helping make folks' vacation to the Shore more enjoyable, and even "the best vacation ever!" We love knowing our book has helped steer people to some of the area's beautiful waterfalls for fun and adventure. Thank you so much for letting us be your guides!

After completing the first edition, we took an unplanned hiatus from North Shore waterfall exploring. Amid the excitement of promoting the book, I experienced a nagging worry that something wasn't quite right. In May of 2006, I was diagnosed with breast cancer. Two surgeries later, I was scheduled to begin chemotherapy. By then, summer was well underway and so was Gary—he'd begun to build me a waterfall in our St. Cloud yard.

For years we had collected large rocks from road and housing construction sites, with the dream of creating two ponds connected by a stepped waterfall cascade. We imagined traffic and neighborhood noise masked by the soothing sound and sight of a rushing, sparkling little stream of waterfalls—a bit of the North Shore in Central Minnesota. Gary decided this was the ideal time to finally tackle the project, so that I could watch the progress from our porch during my months of treatment, adding a bright diversion to what otherwise promised to be a miserable summer.

Well I got my beautiful waterfall, in addition to an unexpected last-minute reprieve from chemotherapy. That wasn't the end of the story, however, and without wasting many more words on medical details, suffice it to say I still had lots of surgeries ahead of me, which ended up stretching over several years. But in 2011, I passed my five-year "cancerversary," at which point the chance of cancer recurrence drops like the High Falls on the Pigeon River. I now enjoy waterfalls even more than before. Each waterfall, like each day, is a treasure.

OUR 10 FAVORITE WATERFALLS

- **Middle Falls** at Gooseberry State Park

- **Beaver River Falls** at Beaver Bay

- **The Cascades** of the Manitou River in Crosby-Manitou State Park

- **Caribou Falls** on the Caribou River

- **Cascade Falls** in Cascade State Park

- **Big Manitou Falls** of the Black River in Pattison State Park, Wisconsin

- **Partridge Falls** of the Pigeon River on the Grand Portage Indian Reservation

- **The High Falls** of the Pigeon River in Grand Portage State Park

- **Kakabeka Falls** in Kakabeka Falls Provincial Park, Ontario

- **Dog Falls** on the Kaministiquia River in Silver Falls Provincial Park, Ontario

BEST HIKES FOR "THE WATERFALL EXPERIENCE"

• Tischer Creek in Duluth's Congdon Park

• Split Rock River at Split Rock Lighthouse State Park

• Temperance River at Temperance River State Park

• Cascade River at Cascade State Park

• Kadunce River at Kadunce River Wayside

• Bad River at Copper Falls State Park, Wisconsin

• Amnicon River at Amnicon Falls State Park, Wisconsin

• Kaministiquia River in Silver Falls Provincial Park, Ontario

Now, after all that water under the bridge, we figured it was high time for a revised and expanded edition of this book. In these intervening years, we've enjoyed many new waterfall encounters, including a few more on "The Shore" that our readers pointed us to, as well as some beyond arbitrary geographic divisions. We wanted to broaden our focus to include some of those waterfalls within day-trip distances of the North Shore.

Who knew we have a 131-foot waterfall known as "The Niagara of the North" less than two hours from Grand Portage? Or the highest waterfall in Wisconsin—comparable to Pigeon River's High Falls—just a half-hour from Duluth? We didn't. But now we do, and after reading this new edition, you will, too!

Postscript: We revisited some of the waterfalls around Duluth, the autumn following the historic flood of June, 2012, afraid we would find some of our favorite trails erased. But what we did find, amazed us. Portions of the Chester Creek trail, for example, had definitely taken a beating. But rebuilding was already well-underway, and we were able to fully enjoy our hike. We headed up to Amity Falls. To our relief, the gazebo still flanked the waterfall. Even the highway bridge between Carlton and Thomson—on the way to Jay Cooke State Park with its Swinging Bridge Falls—has already been re-opened, as well as the park road as far as the visitor's center. Damage to the north pillar of the swinging bridge is slated for repair by late summer of 2013. Happily, we believe that barring any new flooding, everything will be back to normal by the time this second edition makes its splash.

WHAT DO WE CONSIDER A WATERFALL?

Don't laugh. We had this discussion many times before settling on a definition. The term "waterfall" is somewhat subjective. At what point does a rapid become a cascade or how high must a fall be to be worthy of listing and describing? Smaller-sized falls might be significant on a relatively tame river or creek, but seemed less important on rivers with numerous, substantial falls. Over time, about 4 feet became our minimum height to qualify. Falls may also be the sum of several smaller tiers or "steps". Some falls plunge over cliffs as cascades, others slide down bedrock slopes. To address the ambiguity of our definition, we developed the concept of "The Waterfall Experience" ratings. At one point, I think on our third visit to Chester Creek Falls, we noted that whether a waterfall was worthy of our mention also depended upon three other factors: 1) How tired we were, 2) how much film we had left, and 3) how badly we needed modern facilities.

THE "WATERFALL EXPERIENCE" RATINGS

How do you evaluate a waterfall? We believe there is no such thing as a "bad" waterfall. Our ratings are based on the premise that any waterfall is worthy of a visit. However, we will admit that, after an unusually long and difficult hike, some falls did seem rather anticlimactic. We are trying to provide a way to evaluate a potential waterfall adventure based upon the scenic qualities of the falls, your available time, and your hiking ability.

> Jaw-dropping!
> ★★★★★
> Awesome!
> ★★★★
> Pretty dang good
> ★★★
> Cool ★★
> Interesting ★

Many factors contributed to our highly subjective evaluation of the "Waterfall Experience." The criteria evolved as we saw more falls. It would have been easiest to rate waterfalls based only upon the height of the cascade. But we found height was only one factor. Some of the falls were not as high, but the surroundings were so exquisite, or the vantage point for viewing the fall was so spectacular, or the sheer volume of water so impressive, or some configuration of the rocks or cascades so unusual, or the experience of the falls so intimate that many variablese factored into our evaluations. The "Waterfall Experience" rating captures our impressions of the falls better than an objective measurement. We try to describe in our narratives what we considered most noteworthy. We hope you find our ratings a helpful, but by no means conclusive, tool.

Our ratings, from the most impressive "Waterfall Experience" to the least impressive, are listed above. For some rivers we rated individual falls, for others we rated the experience of a series of falls along a stretch of river. In some cases, individual falls distinctly deserved recognition. In other cases, a stretch of river with a series of falls made the trek worthwhile.

DIFFICULTY OF THE HIKE
AND TRAIL QUALITY RATINGS

WHEELCHAIR ACCESSIBLE WATERFALLS

- **Oldenburg Point Cascades Overlook** on the St. Louis River in Jay Cooke State Park

- The **first waterfall** on Miller Creek is visible from a car in Lincoln Park, Duluth

- **Middle Falls** on Gooseberry River in Gooseberry Falls State Park

- **High Falls** on Pigeon River in Grand Portage State Park

- **Cross River Falls** at the Cross River Wayside

- **Kakabeka Falls** on the Kaministiquia River in Kakabeka Falls Provincial Park, Ontario

- **Copper Falls** on the Bad River in Copper Falls State Park, Wisconsin

- **Big Manitou Falls** on the Black River in Pattison State Park, Wisconsin

These two variables are subjective as well, especially difficulty of the hike. Ratings of the quality and strenuousness of the trails are from the viewpoint of a 40-something couple, who are in reasonably good physical shape, and who prefer to hike moderate (1 to 3 miles round trip), but not excessive (4+ miles) distances. Some falls in this book are visible from adjacent parking areas, while others require several hours of hiking.

We found that, as a day of exploring progressed, we greeted stairways with less enthusiasm than we might have first thing in the morning. Or, if it were 85 degrees and sunny, we might be reaching for the water bottle more often than if it were 40 degrees and overcast. Again, many variables influenced our evaluation of strenuousness. Take these obvious factors into account when embarking on your hikes. You may conclude that either we are really wimps, given our ratings, or that we are in much better shape than we think we are. (That would be nice!) Difficulty was greatly influenced by trail quality, distance, and grade of slope. We rated the difficulty of the hike as: Easy, Moderate, or Strenuous.

Trail quality was a more objective factor to evaluate. Some trails are paved and wheelchair accessible. Some are very well trodden dirt or gravel. Some are barely discernable or eroding away. Rocks and large tree roots may make walking difficult. Some trails are fairly level, some have gentle grades, and some are so steep that we swore we would never visit them again! (Invariably, that was where our photos didn't turn out well and we needed to revisit them several times.) Some stairways are well-constructed with wood railings, some are masterfully crafted with fitted stone, some utilize conveniently spaced tree-roots, and some are poorly maintained railroad ties pulling away from the banks. Taking all of these factors into account, we rated trail quality as: Good, Fair, or Poor.

HIKING TIMES ALONG THE TRAILS

How long it takes someone to walk to any of the waterfalls featured in this book will vary widely, depending upon the individual. Often we report how much time it took us to reach different points along the trail, to help clarify and lend perspective to our directions. Use our estimated times as a reference rather than as a rule. Timing is based not only on how fast you hike, but also upon how often you stop to smell the flowers or linger to enjoy the view. Sometimes it took us much longer to get to a falls than to get back—the lollygag factor. Surprisingly, this was almost always the case, even though we had more energy starting out than when we returned. We generally walk a mile in about 15 to 30 minutes, depending upon the terrain. See how our walking times compare with yours and adjust accordingly.

THE EVER-CHANGING NATURE OF WATERFALLS

As we learned by visiting and photographing many water-falls, you can return to the same falls at different times of the year or even at different times of the day, and have a new experience. A waterfall that was tumultuous in April may be a trickle in August. This is not necessarily a bad thing. Lower water levels may reveal previously invisible rock formations or may provide closer access to the falls than is possible during spring thaw.

River water levels are more or less variable depending upon their source. Some rivers have headwaters—lakes, wet-lands, streams, or springs that provide consistent flow. Other rivers depend upon runoff from rain and snowmelt. All of the rivers have high flows in the spring and after heavy rains. Spring offers dramatic flows, but a lush summer backdrop may add more beauty to the scene than loads of water. As you move farther up the shore, more rivers are fed by lakes, making their flow less changeable with the season.

Another factor to consider is time of day. A morning visit to Amity Falls may reward you with rainbows shifting in the mist at its base. Late in the day, deep shadows may lend a

BEST SECRET WATERFALLS

- West Branch Split Rock River Falls

- Unnamed falls on the way to Barrier Falls of Devil Track River

- Shovel Point Falls on the Baptism River

- Cut Face Creek Waterfall

- Unnamed falls on a Cascade River tributary

- Table Rock Waterfall on an unnamed creek flowing into the Manitou River

- Morgan Creek Falls, Wisconsin

- Little Falls in Kakabeka Falls Provincial Park, Ontario

mysterious air to the setting. Many of the North Shore falls flow within steep-walled canyons, with little sun permeating the deep shade, while a few others, such as the Pigeon River's High Falls, bask in the sun most of the day.

With so many variables, it is impossible to predict how a falls will look until you see it. That's part of the allure of waterfalls.

TIPS FOR WATERFALL SEEKERS

Numerous books address the fine points of hiking safety, etiquette, and what supplies to take with you. We will trust your common sense and other sources to cover these topics. There are, however, some items which we recommend taking with you.

For instance, always bring drinking water. You may figure, "The trail is well marked. This is a short hike. I don't need to take water with me." Wrong! The worst situation is to negotiate a long stretch of steps on a hot July day and see and hear ice cold water everywhere…but not have a drop to drink. A fanny pack with water and a snack bar is always welcome on the trail.

Apply the sunscreen before you set out and bring along some insect repellant. Often, the bug dope is totally unnecessary, but it's smart to have it with you, just in case. It's always nice to have a light jacket for those cool northern Minnesota mornings and that fickle North Shore weather. Every so often, you hear about someone getting lost in a state park. It is highly doubtful that any of these hikes will result in your becoming lost, but since we prefer to be overly cautious, we always pack a state park map, if available, a compass, and matches. Enclose your camera in a zip-lock bag. Stow extra shoes and socks in the car. Bring newspaper to put on the floor of your car, in case your clothes or footgear become muddy or wet.

Always use common sense. Know your limits. Stop to smell the wild roses. And be sure to savor the "Waterfall Experience."

WATERFALLS CHECKLIST

Minnesota

St. Louis River
- ☐ Swinging Bridge Falls
- ☐ Oldenburg Point Cascades

Kingsbury Creek Falls
- ☐ Kingsbury Creek Falls

Keene Creek
- ☐ Blue Nude Falls
- ☐ Other Keene Creek Falls

Miller Creek
- ☐ Miller Creek Falls

Chester Creek
- ☐ Chester Creek Falls

Tischer Creek
- ☐ Tischer Creek Falls

Amity Creek
- ☐ Amity Creek Falls
- ☐ Keep Smiling Falls
- ☐ The Deep Falls

Lester River
- ☐ Japp Hole Falls
- ☐ Gunderson's Falls
- ☐ Shallows Falls
- ☐ Nude Swimming Hole Falls
- ☐ Two Sisters Falls

French River
- ☐ French River Falls

Schmidt Creek
- ☐ Schmidt Creek Falls

Sucker River
- ☐ Sucker River Falls

Knife River
- ☐ First Falls
- ☐ Second Falls

Gooseberry River
- ☐ Lower Falls
- ☐ Middle Falls
- ☐ Upper Falls
- ☐ Fifth Falls

Nelsens Creek
- ☐ Nelsens Creek Falls

Split Rock River
- ☐ West Branch Falls
- ☐ First Falls
- ☐ White Falls
- ☐ Two-Step Falls
- ☐ Red Falls
- ☐ The Slide
- ☐ Upper Slide Falls
- ☐ Island Falls
- ☐ Split Rock Falls
- ☐ Orange Falls

Beaver River
- ☐ Beaver River Falls
- ☐ South Camp Falls
- ☐ Glen Avon Falls

Baptism River
- ☐ Shovel Point Falls
- ☐ The Cascades
- ☐ Two Step Falls
- ☐ High Falls
- ☐ Illgen Falls

Manitou River
- ☐ The Cascades
- ☐ Riding Rock Falls
- ☐ Table Rock Falls
- ☐ Dam Falls
- ☐ Mouth of the Manitou
- ☐ Other Manitou River Falls

Caribou River
- ☐ Caribou Falls
- ☐ More Caribou River Falls

Crystal Creek
- ☐ Crystal Creek Falls

Two Island River
- ☐ Lower Two Island Falls
- ☐ Upper Two Island Falls

Cross River
- ☐ Cross River Falls
- ☐ Other Cross River Falls

Temperance River
- ☐ Hidden Falls
- ☐ Upper Falls
- ☐ Lower Falls
- ☐ The Cauldron
- ☐ Other Temperance River Falls

Onion River
- ☐ Onion River Falls

Poplar River
- ☐ Upper Falls
- ☐ Middle Falls
- ☐ Lower Falls

Cascade River
- ☐ Cascade Falls
- ☐ The Cascades
- ☐ More Cascade River Falls
- ☐ Secret Waterfall
- ☐ Hidden Falls
- ☐ Thompson Falls

Cut Face Creek
- ☐ Cut Face Creek Falls

Fall River
- ☐ Fall River Falls

Devil Track River
- ☐ Devil Track Falls

- ☐ Barrier Falls

Kadunce River
- ☐ Kadunce River Falls
- ☐ Heart of the Earth Falls

Brule River
- ☐ Devil's Kettle
- ☐ Upper Falls

Pigeon River
- ☐ High Falls
- ☐ Upper Middle Falls
- ☐ Lower Middle Falls
- ☐ Partridge Falls

Ontario

Current River
- ☐ Trowbridge Falls
- ☐ Sevigney Creek Falls
- ☐ The Cascades

Kaministiquia River
- ☐ Kakabeka Falls
- ☐ Little Falls
- ☐ Unnamed Falls
- ☐ Dog Falls

Cedar Creek
- ☐ Cedar Creek Falls

MacKenzie River
- ☐ MacKenzie Falls

Upper Wolf River
- ☐ Lower Falls

Wisconsin

Black River
- ☐ Big Manitou Falls
- ☐ Little Manitou Falls

Amnicon River
- ☐ Upper Falls
- ☐ Lower Falls
- ☐ The Snake Pit Falls
- ☐ Now & Then Falls

Morgan Creek
- ☐ Morgan Creek Falls

Tyler Forks and Bad Rivers
- ☐ Brownstone Falls
- ☐ Cascades
- ☐ Copper Falls
- ☐ Red Granite Falls

Potato River
- ☐ Lower Falls
- ☐ Upper Falls
- ☐ Foster Falls

Montreal River
- ☐ Superior Falls
- ☐ Saxon Falls
- ☐ Interstate Falls

Minnesota Waterfalls

Minnesota's North Shore offers so much—Lake Superior glints crystal against rugged, rocky cliffs and stone-strewn beaches. High emerald hills roll up from the shore into wilderness haunts of moose, bear and wolf. By wing—and by voice—gulls, ravens, and eagles slice the sky, and icy rivers collide and slide through high, shadowed canyons of rust and black. We'll be taking you into those canyons.

The striking scenery of this area, including its resplendent waterfalls, arose due to dramatic geologic events over many millions, even billions, of years. These included volcanic eruptions, magma flows, gargantuan grinding glaciers, and massive melts. Many of the parks in which the wild rivers dance feature fascinating interpretive materials that tell the stories of their formation.

Our exploration, in this section of the book, begins at the St. Louis River, just south of Duluth, and follows the shore of Lake Superior to the Canadian border. Conveniently, all of the described falls, except for those in Jay Cooke State Park, occur within just a few miles of both the lake and the North Shore's famous Highway 61.

There are so many must-see waterfalls along the North Shore. We outlined some of them in the introduction. We were surprised not only by how many waterfalls exist, but also how minimally they are noted in some of the parks—even in parks where certain waterfalls are featured and after which the park is named. Others—virtually ignored—don't even show up on the state park maps. And some rivers, popular only with anglers, contain lovely waterfalls that few people other than fishermen know exist.

The North Shore hikes described in this book offer magnificent scenery and experiences of many kinds, but what we enjoy most is the thunder building as we near the falls, the anticipation of seeing white water through the trees, and the discovery of waterfalls great and small. It is never disappointing.

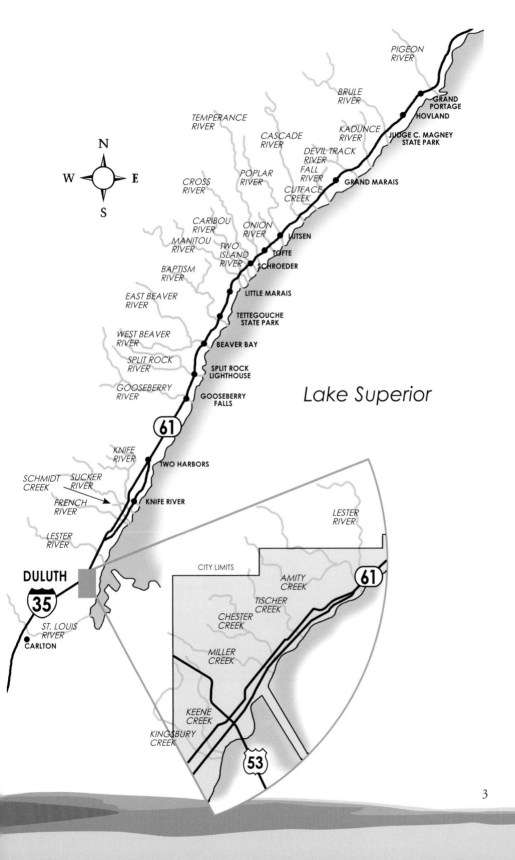

N W E S

PIGEON
RIVER

BRULE
RIVER

GRAND
PORTAGE

HOVLAND

TEMPERANCE
RIVER

KADUNCE
RIVER

JUDGE C. MAGNEY
STATE PARK

CASCADE
RIVER

DEVIL TRACK
RIVER

FALL
RIVER

CROSS
RIVER

POPLAR
RIVER

CUTFACE
CREEK

GRAND MARAIS

CARIBOU
RIVER

ONION
RIVER

LUTSEN

MANITOU
RIVER

TWO
ISLAND
RIVER

TOFTE

BAPTISM
RIVER

SCHROEDER

LITTLE MARAIS

EAST BEAVER
RIVER

TETTEGOUCHE
STATE PARK

WEST BEAVER
RIVER

BEAVER BAY

SPLIT ROCK
RIVER

SPLIT ROCK
LIGHTHOUSE

GOOSEBERRY
RIVER

GOOSEBERRY
FALLS

Lake Superior

61

KNIFE
RIVER

TWO HARBORS

SCHMIDT
CREEK

SUCKER
RIVER

FRENCH
RIVER

KNIFE RIVER

LESTER
RIVER

LESTER
RIVER

DULUTH

CITY LIMITS

AMITY
CREEK

61

35

TISCHER
CREEK

ST. LOUIS
RIVER

CHESTER
CREEK

CARLTON

MILLER
CREEK

KEENE
CREEK

KINGSBURY
CREEK

53

3

Swinging Bridge Falls

St. Louis River
Jay Cooke State Park, Carlton

Swinging Bridge Falls

TRAILHEAD: Swinging Bridge Falls is in Jay Cooke State Park, located 10 miles southwest of Duluth. To access the park from I-35, take exit 239 and follow State Highway 45 east to Carlton. In Carlton, turn left on Highway 210 (Chester Avenue) and go a little over 2 miles to the state park entrance. One and a half miles into the park, turn right into the River Inn visitor center parking lot. The falls are located directly behind the visitor center.

HIKE DIFFICULTY
Easy
TRAIL QUALITY
Good
ROUND TRIP
0.25 miles
THE EXPERIENCE
★★★

The geology shaping the falls on the St. Louis River differs markedly from that of the North Shore. Here, huge sheets of slate lean at dramatic angles with water coursing over and between them, resulting in myriad waterfalls. Swinging Bridge Falls is one of the largest.

The crazily tilted rock formations you see today were once mud deposits which, over two billion years of heat and pressure, compacted first into shale and then into Thomson slate. The slate folded and cracked from eons of underground movement and pressure. Molten rock later squeezed through these cracks to create diabase dikes. The river generally flows along the slate folds, but where the river bends, the water flows across the folds, forming falls. Other falls came about where the slate has eroded.

A delightful group of falls is visible from the Swinging Bridge—a suspension bridge just behind the visitor center—as well as from the shore and various spots along riverside hiking trails. An arrowhead-shaped island divides the river flow just upstream from the bridge. Swinging Bridge Falls are on the left side, plunging about 12 feet.

On the right side of the island is another series of falls. Walk a short distance upstream on the visitor center side of the bridge to a large clearing with scattered picnic tables and benches. From there you can see small cascades flowing at every possible angle, including some flowing upstream. This collection of cascades is more or less visible due to the volume of water flowing through the gorge, which varies from a torrent to a trickle depending upon the season.

If you are nimble, take a small path down to another rock terrace, where a slate wall about 4 feet high creates a barrier between you and the river. The rock has amazing acoustical properties that block out the steady roar of the St. Louis River, while providing a closer view of the turbulence below. If you visit the falls on a gusty day, you may see gobs of foam tossed into the air like soapsuds blown from a child's hand.

Oldenburg Point Cascades

HIKE DIFFICULTY
Easy, wheelchair accessible overlook. Strenuous to river level.

TRAIL QUALITY
Good to overlook
Fair to cascades

ROUND TRIP
0.5 mile to overlook
0.7 mile to cascades

THE EXPERIENCE
★ ★ ★

TRAILHEAD: Turn right onto Highway 210 from the Jay Cooke State Park River Inn visitor center parking lot. About 1 mile from the visitor center is the parking lot and picnic area for Oldenburg Point. Park here. The paved trailhead to the overlook begins from the middle of the parking lot and is clearly marked. From the overlook, a short, strenuous trail goes down to the river and cascades.

Follow the paved path a quarter mile to an overlook of the St. Louis River Cascades. These cascades are not shown on the state park map. We don't know why. While Swinging Bridge Falls is a lovely falls and may be higher than most of the scores of falls in this wild and wooly section of the St. Louis River, we think the Oldenburg Point Cascades are truly awesome. You'll see why when you reach the overlook. Almost a mile of rapids and falls stretch up and down river, producing a thunderous roar of incredible volume. Especially savage in the spring, the Oldenburg Cascades are set against the backdrop of steep forested hills.

The difficult decision is whether to brave the short, well-constructed, but wicked trail from the overlook down to the river's edge. What makes it wicked? One hundred and seventy-seven steps, 56 of which are slate, the rest built of railroad ties. The series of steps are connected by a descending dirt path in fair condition. When you get to the bottom, the trail goes left along the rocks and is difficult to discern.

Oldenburg Point Cascades

At water's edge, you'll behold a huge volume of white water churning around and over gigantic boulders. This misty maelstrom is a rapids of gargantuan scale. Falls range from about 10 to 15 feet in height, and the cataracts span the wide river. Find a seat at water's edge. If you can hear yourself think, the mighty St. Louis will put your own limited power into perspective. If this doesn't leave you humbled, the 177 steps back up to the parking lot will.

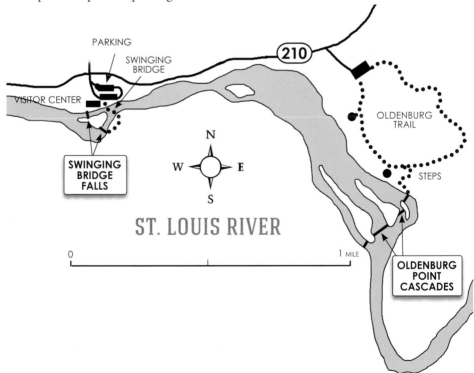

Kingsbury Creek Falls by the Zoo

KINGSBURY CREEK
Fairmont Park / Duluth Zoo, Duluth

Kingsbury Creek Falls

TRAILHEAD: Coming from the south, take exit 251 off of I-35 onto Cody Street. Following the signs to the Lake Superior Zoo, turn right on North 63rd Avenue South and then right on Grand Avenue. Turn right again on 71st Avenue West and take the left fork onto Fremont Street. Park in the Lake Superior Zoo lot, at 72nd Avenue West and Fremont Street. Coming from the north, exit off of I-35 on Highway 23, which is Grand Avenue. Once on Grand Avenue, follow the same directions as above.

HIKE DIFFICULTY
Strenuous
TRAIL QUALITY
Poor
ROUND TRIP
1.3 miles
THE EXPERIENCE
★★

At the west end of the parking lot, across the gravel road from the playground equipment, descend 27 steps to the pavilion building. From the right end of the building, you get a good view of Kingsbury Creek as it drops down the hillside over smooth red bedrock, passing under two bridges, in a series of small falls. This long stretch of cascading water is an impressive vista when the creek is high.

Go back to the wide gravel road and follow it to the end. The road is bordered on the left by a chain-link fence. Continue on the path along the fence as it wraps around the boundary of the zoo in a gradual arch to the left. In about 50 yards, you will intersect another gravel road. Go left on this road and you will soon see a yellow metal gate under an old, stone-arched railroad bridge. Pass under this bridge and you will immediately see a sign saying "Kingsbury Trail—1.3 miles." At this point, the trail splits. Go left and you will very shortly come to the creek.

The tall pink, blue, and lavender stalks of lupines, *among the most prolific and beautiful wildflowers along North Shore highways in the summer, are named after the Latin word for "wolf." They're so named because of the misconception that they cause the poor quality soil where they live.*

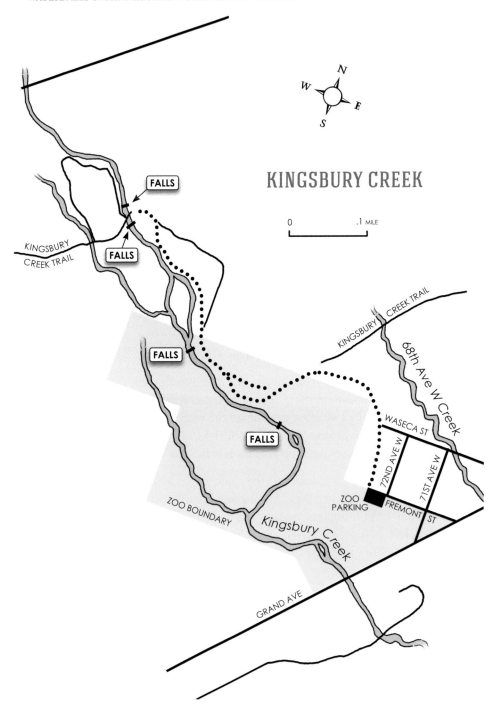

KINGSBURY CREEK

From here, walk upstream on the east side of the creek on the dirt and rock path. In a few minutes, you will come to another bridge. You can enjoy the view from the bridge, but stay on the path on the east side. In a few minutes you will find a short spur path down to the creek, where a small waterfall squeezes past large, graffiti-covered rock outcroppings. Continuing onward, return to the path.

The path, now sand, begins to veer away from the water. Don't follow this. Instead, follow an informal grass path along the creek. The surrounding forest contains many deciduous trees, making for a lovely stroll. There are also conifers, including some stray cedars. About five minutes beyond the graffiti-decorated outcropping are more falls several feet in height. The path rises. Five railroad-tie steps have been placed to aid your climb. Look for a left spur, just before a large, flat-faced boulder to the left of the trail, leading down to a picturesque spot on a rock promontory overlooking another series of small, three-stepped cascades with pools in between.

Just above these cascades is an old footbridge. An orange arrow at the bridge indicates that Kingsbury Creek Nature Trail continues across this bridge and away from the creek. Stay on the east side of the creek instead. A waterfall flows in a narrow ribbon of water, only 1 to 2 feet wide, along a central fissure in the creek bed. Viewed from the bridge, it continues in steps as far as you can see.

Two paths head upstream on the east side of the creek. Take the one nearest the creek. In about two minutes you will come to a spur leading to yet another series of cascades. This may be the tallest cascade on the creek, as the falls seem to tumble down and down and down, with no end in sight. In places gravity and the rock fissures appear at odds, as though the creek and rock have different intentions.

Very shortly another spur leads to the creek. It is a well-worn dirt path and the view of the small falls at this point is not worth the hike down and back up, in our humble opinion. As you continue along, you will hear traffic and see, at the top of the hill, the tall chain-link fence that marks the edge of the freeway and the turnaround point for your Kingsbury Creek waterfall tour.

Marsh marigold, *also known as cowslip, is a vivid yellow spring wildflower of wetlands and along streams. Blooms are 1 to 2 inches across, and leaves are rounded, leathery, and avoided by cattle and deer.*

Blue Nude Falls

KEENE CREEK
Skyline Drive, Duluth

Blue Nude Falls

TRAILHEAD: Coming from downtown Duluth, take I-35 south and get off at the 40th Avenue West exit. The exit brings you to Michigan Street, which runs into 40th. Go right on 40th to Grand Avenue. Go left on Grand Avenue West to 57th Avenue. Turn right on 57th and follow it to Highland Street. Turn left on Highland and the first right after Oneota Cemetery is Skyline Drive. Turn right on Skyline Drive and park immediately on the west side of Skyline in a dirt turnoff area. If you are coming from the south on I-35, take the Cody Street exit. Follow Cody to 57th Avenue West, where you turn left. The directions from here are the same as above. The trailhead is located across Skyline from the parking area, just left of the 30 mph speed limit sign.

HIKE DIFFICULTY
Moderate/
Strenuous if you
go down to
the creek

TRAIL QUALITY
Poor

ROUND TRIP
< 0.1 mile

THE EXPERIENCE
★★

Follow the gravel path about 50 feet to the remains of an old concrete bridge. A very poor, very steep dirt path to the right of the bridge goes down to the waterfall, which is beneath the bridge. You can climb down to the creek level on this path or instead, and much easier, just as you pass around the concrete wall of the bridge, go to the right and view the waterfall from the riverbank. The Blue Nude Falls is directly under the old bridge and has a drop of approximately 8 feet into a small pool. It is surrounded by vertical rock walls adorned with various graffiti, including a rendering of a blue nude, hence the name. This is definitely an urban waterfall; the defaced surroundings are unfortunately strewn with broken glass and pieces of trash.

On your waterfall hikes, you may occasionally come upon a wild rose *bush in a forest opening. Fewer petaled than its cultivated cousin, the flowers produce red berries known as "rose hips," which are high in vitamin C and can serve as an ingredient in tea.*

A nice spot on Keene Creek

...*more* Keene Creek Falls

TRAILHEAD: From the intersection of Highland Street and Skyline Drive, drive 0.3 mile east on Skyline Drive. There is a small dirt turnoff on the right where you can park.

The waterfall is located only a minute from the road, down a small dirt and gravel path. The 5-foot waterfall is surrounded by ferns and moss-covered rocks. While modest by North Shore standards, if it were someone's water garden, it would be spectacular. What a nice spot to picnic!

HIKE DIFFICULTY
Easy

TRAIL QUALITY
Good

ROUND TRIP
< 0.1 mile

THE EXPERIENCE
★

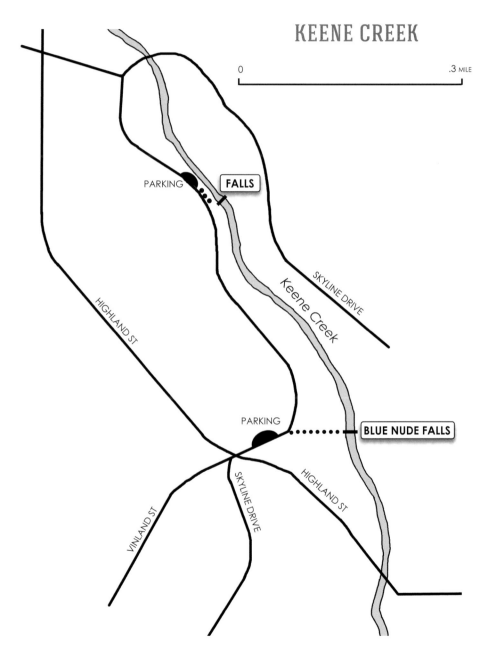

KEENE CREEK

0   .3 MILE

PARKING   **FALLS**

SKYLINE DRIVE

Keene Creek

HIGHLAND ST

PARKING   **BLUE NUDE FALLS**

SKYLINE DRIVE

HIGHLAND ST

VINLAND ST

Falls at Lincoln Park Entrance

MILLER CREEK
Lincoln Park, Duluth

Miller Creek Falls

TRAILHEAD: From I-35, take exit 254, and head uphill on 27th Avenue West. Turn right on West 3rd Street and in one block you will see Lincoln Park. At the next corner, where 3rd intersects with 25th Avenue West, turn left into the park entrance on Lincoln Park Drive.

HIKE DIFFICULTY
Easy
TRAIL QUALITY
Good to Fair
ROUND TRIP
all <0.1 mile
from your car
THE EXPERIENCE
★ to ★ ★ ★

We were pleasantly surprised by the Miller Creek waterfall experience. It is a very active creek, with numerous falls and cascades along its route. All are easily accessible from the road along the creek.

Lincoln Park was one of Duluth's first four parks, established in 1889. As you enter the park, you will see its most unusual waterfall. We found it unusual because it is a "tamed" waterfall, in the midst of a highly groomed section of city park, where Miller Creek is bound by constructed rock walls. Picnic tables pepper the lawn up to water's edge. There is even a playground just across the road from the falls. This waterfall looks uncomfortable to us, as though it really wants to be somewhere else—somewhere surrounded by cliffs and pines. The incongruity is both interesting and unsettling. A metal bridge spans the top of the falls, where the creek is approximately 20 feet wide. The creek drops about 30 feet as it slides 150 feet over a smooth rock run, widening as it goes.

Following the road, about 0.2 mile from the park entrance, is another waterfall. Now you've already seen a tamed waterfall, so you can better appreciate this one. This 6-foot drop is unique. It flows through a 4-foot gully, hits one side of the creek channel, turns left 90 degrees, then makes a tight-angled right turn, before finally

Bloodroot is a less common, early spring wildflower. Found in moist, deciduous woods, 8 to 12 white petals surround a yellow stamen. Its orange-red juice, which was used by Native Americans for dye and war paint, resides not only in the root, as the name would suggest, but throughout the plant.

17

passing beneath a small concrete bridge.

At 0.4 mile from the park entrance, another footbridge spans Miller Creek. From the bridge (which has very widely spaced railings—be careful with children), you can look up and downstream to see a series of cascades and falls skipping through a narrow gully lined with evergreen, birch, and dogwood. Miller Creek is now free of its urban confines. At this point, a nice hiking path goes along the opposite side of the creek from the road. At 0.5 mile, a 6-foot waterfall is visible from the road, along

Upper Falls on Miller Creek

with cascades which run for over 100 yards. At 0.6 mile, there is a parking turnout for a 4-foot waterfall, running over red rock and beneath a picturesque old stone bridge.

We consider the best falls in Lincoln Park to be at the 0.7 mile mark. The setting is natural, with large boulders and old willow trees leaning out over the creek. Below the falls, water flows around a rocky island. The cataract is about 10 feet high and moss carpets the rock at its base. A large, flat rock outcrop that juts into the creek below the falls is a nice place to meditate.

The much sought-after Lake Superior agate *has been the official Minnesota gemstone since 1969. Formed in and around Lake Superior during volcanic eruptions a billion years ago, they were distributed over Minnesota and Wisconsin during glacial activity 10,000 - 15,000 years ago.*

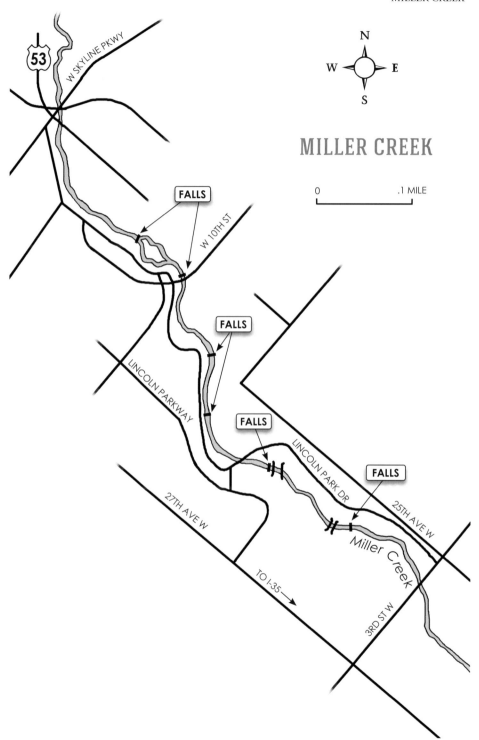

MILLER CREEK

0 .1 MILE

Chester Creek Falls

CHESTER CREEK
Chester Park, Duluth

Chester Creek Falls

TRAILHEAD: In Duluth, follow Skyline Drive to the park entrance on Chester Bowl Drive. Turn right into the park and there is parking immediately inside. Park here and walk back across Skyline Drive. The trailhead is by the Chester Creek Park sign on the northeast side of the Skyline Drive bridge.

HIKE DIFFICULTY
Moderate
TRAIL QUALITY
Fair
ROUND TRIP
2.5 miles
THE EXPERIENCE
★ ★

The park contains 2.5 miles of hiking trails and is a startling contrast to its urban surroundings. Chester Creek winds through a steep, northwoods ravine shaded by tall pines. The peaceful sight and sound of flowing water allow the bustle of the city to drop away. Along the creek you'll find lady and maidenhair ferns, wild strawberries, thimbleberries, blue-bead lilies and seven waterfalls. Our walking time was about one hour along the east side of the river (with much stopping to take photos and explore side trails), and half an hour back up the other side (with little lollygagging).

From the trailhead, follow a short flight of steps down to the first waterfall. The gradual, 40-foot-long slide is a fitting introduction to the treasures of this creek. Approximately 40 yards downstream is an impressive series of cascades that while not of great volume, split, rejoin, and split again, dropping about 30 feet.

The trail quality is generally good—not too steep, nor too rocky. Two footbridges cross the creek, with steep staircases ascending from the bridges to street level; reminders that civilization is just steps (though quite a few) away. There is a 10-foot waterfall beneath the first footbridge, where steps climb to the intersection of 17th Avenue East and Chester Park Drive. Many side trails head off for closer views of the water, but the main trail is always clearly discernable.

Chester Creek *gets its name from an 1850s pioneer, Charles Chester.*

One of Chester Creek's waterfalls

Continuing downstream, you walk beneath a concrete underpass to reach the second footbridge, which straddles a narrow channel and has steps ascending on the other side to 14th Avenue East and 6th Street. Here the evergreens begin to give way to deciduous trees. The noises of the city re-emerge at the eastern boundary of Chester Creek Park—the bridge at 14th Avenue East and East 4th Street—an impressive, red-capped, stone structure from which you get a great view of three falls. One pours into a round pool, which feeds two more falls before the creek flows beneath the bridge.

Return upstream on the west side for a different perspective. The west bank has a more gradual slope, so the trail is closer to the water. You can see several small waterfalls and rocky bluffs that you missed on the way down.

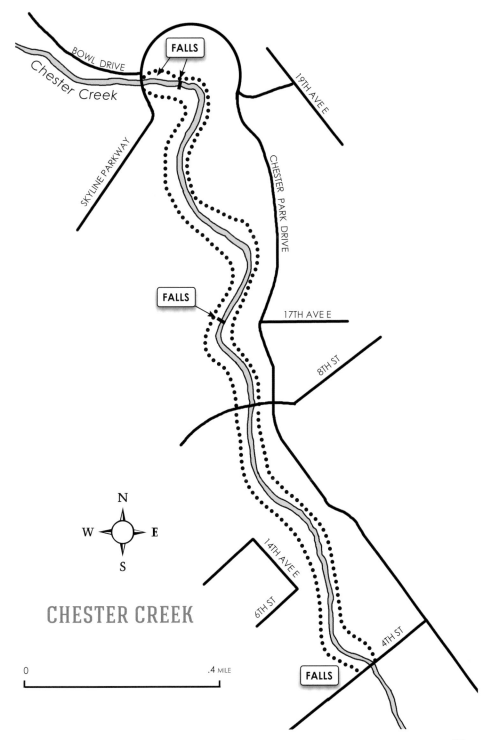

BOWL DRIVE

Chester Creek

FALLS

19TH AVE E

SKYLINE PARKWAY

CHESTER PARK DRIVE

FALLS

17TH AVE E

8TH ST

N
W E
S

14TH AVE E

6TH ST

CHESTER CREEK

4TH ST

FALLS

0 .4 MILE

Upper Falls on Tischer Creek

TISCHER CREEK
Congdon Park, Duluth

Tischer Creek Falls

TRAILHEAD: From Highway 61 (London Road) turn left (north) on 32nd Avenue East (just before the Glensheen Mansion) which runs into Congdon Park Drive. Follow this to the right for two blocks and cross Superior Street. You will see Congdon Park immediately on your right. Park along the road. The trail to the waterfalls begins at the corner of Superior Street and Congdon Park Drive near the Congdon Park sign.

HIKE DIFFICULTY
Moderate
TRAIL QUALITY
Poor to Good
ROUND TRIP
1.5 miles
THE EXPERIENCE
★★★ to
★★★★

Tischer Creek and its five major waterfalls lie within Congdon Park, a 34-acre piece of paradise that was donated by prominent Duluthian Chester Congdon in the early 1900s. While the scale of the falls is not as grand as some of the more popular falls farther up "The Shore," its fairytale-like environs provide an unexpectedly intimate waterfall experience. High water flows definitely heighten the experience, but at no time of year have we failed to be enchanted by this park.

Enter Congdon Park at the dirt trail and descend the stone steps by the bridge. (There is also a gray gravel trail that parallels Tischer Creek, but it goes higher up the bank and you miss the first few waterfalls.) The stone steps lead you into a red chasm shaded beneath a canopy of maples. Heading upstream, you will encounter the first of several footbridges zig-zagging across the meandering creek. The contrast of the red rock framed with lush, emerald-green moss is stunning. Tall pines and cedars grow here. We even glimpsed a great blue heron. Just past the second bridge,

In spring you may find columbine, *with its distinctive orange and yellow flowers, blooming in less dense areas of the forest or in rocky areas along rivers. Its name derives from the Latin word for dove, "columba." If you have a good imagination, the flower is said to resemble a flock of these birds.*

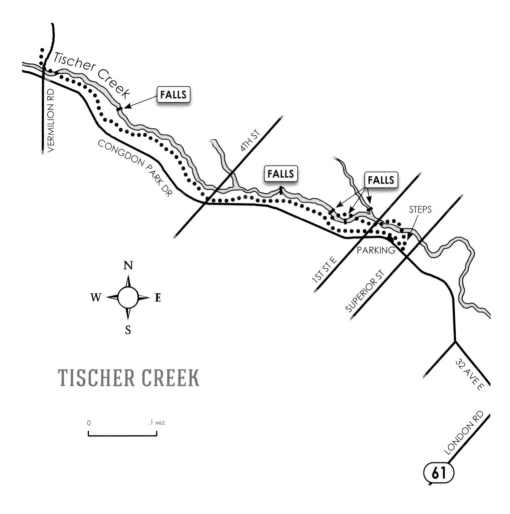

TISCHER CREEK

on your right, an unexpected and dramatic 15-foot tributary cascade drops from the cliff above and into the creek. Like falling lace, the water gently bounces among the myriad of fissures and cracks in the rock face.

You cross over Tischer Creek twice on the footbridges. The creek slides beneath you, gradually dropping approximately 25 feet and making a 180-degree turn in the process. Immediately upstream is the second waterfall. It tumbles about 30 feet over three steps, in a gentle turn, coming to rest in a small reflecting pool. Be sure to note the master craftsmanship of the builders of the path. Stone staircases appear to be carved from the rock itself, but close inspection reveals how rocks were fitted and cemented into place. The path, soft with pine needles, is often lined on each side with carefully placed river boulders. A few minutes of walking brings you to the third waterfall, which begins as a narrow chute, but hits a small pool and then broadens and slides as it completes three 90-degree turns. The view from the base is awesome, the falls run directly toward you, then take a final right turn.

A leisurely, half-hour stroll from the trailhead brings you about 0.3 miles to the 4th Street bridge. Cross 4th Street and the trail continues from a sign stating "Congdon Park 1.5 mile hiking trail." Again, you can choose between the gray gravel path above the creek and the creek-side trail, which is rougher but more satisfying. Take the creek trail to enjoy the beautiful stonework and get up close and personal with the

Waterfall on Tischer Creek in Congdon Park

creek. This upper stretch of Tischer Creek has many gentle drops along its course. The first major waterfall you see is made up of four terraces. Then, five minutes farther up the trail—just as you think this upper stretch may be tamer—a striking, 30-foot stepped cascade comes to view. Water tumbles here and there over jagged rocks, encircling a small, craggy island. Where sunlight finds it way to the creek, long waves of bright green algae dance in the torrent, though high water may obscure the underwater flora. Walk on and 15 minutes later you will reach the trail's end at the bridge at Vermillion Road and East St. Marie Street. You can choose from three parallel paths for your walk back. One is suitable for car traffic, but closed off. The gray trail is a biking path. And there is the trail along the creek. If you take either of the upper paths, you will miss much of the scenery but can cover the whole distance back to your car in about 15 minutes.

Crusty *("Crustose")* lichens *of many different types are common on rock outcrops along North Shore rivers. These are long-lived, sun-loving plants that are actually composed of two kinds of plants joined in a symbiotic relationship—a fungus and an alga. The fungus is most visible and provides water and minerals for the alga, while the alga makes carbohydrates needed by the fungus.*

Amity Falls

AMITY CREEK
Lester Park, Duluth

Amity Falls

TRAILHEAD: Amity Falls is located on Amity Creek, a western branch of the Lester River. To get to Amity Falls from Highway 61, also called London Road, turn left (north) onto 60th Avenue East. Go two blocks to Superior Street and turn right. Just before the Lester River bridge, turn left onto Occidental Boulevard. Follow Occidental 0.4 mile, crossing Amity Creek on an old stone bridge. Immediately after crossing the bridge, park in a small turn off. The short trail to Amity Falls begins here.

HIKE DIFFICULTY
Easy
TRAIL QUALITY
Good
ROUND TRIP
<0.1 miles
THE EXPERIENCE
★ ★ ★

Walk downstream on the east side of Amity Creek. In a minute, after passing two small falls, you will reach a footbridge just above Amity Falls, which leads to a gazebo on the opposite bank. Cross Amity Creek on the footbridge and you can look down on the falls. Make your way down the rocks on the west side, to the base of the falls. Looking up at Amity Falls, the creek squeezes out from a notch in the basalt wall, plummeting 20 feet down a rocky face. The large pool at the bottom is named "The Deeps" by locals.

More Amity Creek Falls

From Amity Falls, Occidental Boulevard becomes Seven Bridges Road, named for the stone bridges spanning Amity Creek. It's a lovely drive, and we recommend stopping to view waterfalls along the way. Drive up Seven Bridges Road, 0.4 mile beyond the bridge near Amity Falls. You will be high above the creek. Park about 100 feet before the second stone bridge and look down to see an unusual three

HIKE DIFFICULTY
Easy
TRAIL QUALITY
Good
ROUND TRIP
Both <0.1 miles
THE EXPERIENCE
★ ★ to ★ ★ ★

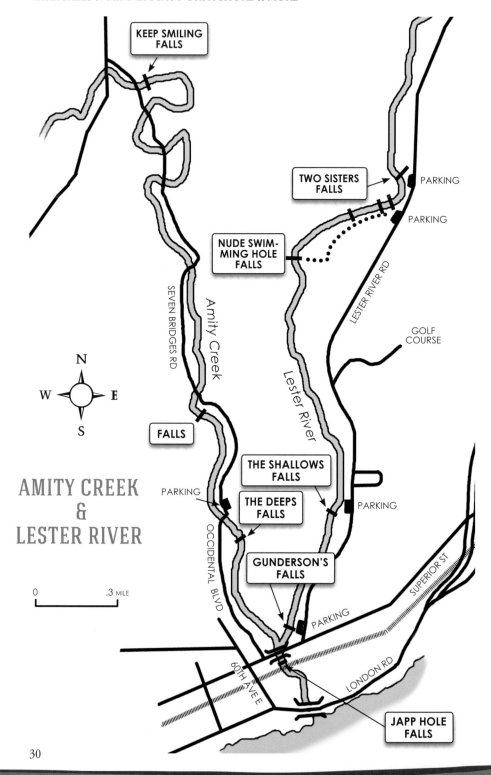

KEEP SMILING
FALLS

TWO SISTERS
FALLS

PARKING

PARKING

NUDE SWIM-
MING HOLE
FALLS

SEVEN BRIDGES RD

Amity Creek

LESTER RIVER RD

GOLF
COURSE

Lester River

N

W   E

S

FALLS

AMITY CREEK
&
LESTER RIVER

THE SHALLOWS
FALLS

PARKING

THE DEEPS
FALLS

PARKING

OCCIDENTAL BLVD

GUNDERSON'S
FALLS

SUPERIOR ST

0   .3 MILE

PARKING

60TH AVE E

LONDON RD

JAPP HOLE
FALLS

Keep Smiling Falls

or four-fingered falls (depending on the water level) with a drop of about 5 feet. A steep, narrow dirt path goes down to the river level, but the view from above is best.

Continuing up Seven Bridges Road, you will pass over stone bridges numbers 3 through 6. Just before bridge 7, about 1.4 miles beyond the first bridge, you can pull off on either side of the road. You may see other cars parked here. Several walking paths lead to outcrops on the river's edge and to a place locals refer to as "Keep Smiling Falls," so-named because of a graffiti message inscribed on a rock face decades ago beneath a smiley face. It is still visible, and we are told that the faded text reads, "Smile. It adds to your face value." This series of falls begins just above the bridge in a string of smaller cascades. Below the bridge, the creek drops about 12 feet. The river pauses in a pool before dashing by the 20th-century petroglyph and cascading another 6 feet into a lower pool.

Shallows Waterfall

LESTER RIVER
Lester Park, Duluth

Japp Hole Falls

TRAILHEAD: From London Road, turn left on 60th Avenue East. Go about two blocks to Superior Street and turn right. Cross the Lester River and turn left (north) on Lester River Road. The main Lester Park parking lot is on the left. Note: See map for Amity Creek on page 30.

HIKE DIFFICULTY
Easy
TRAIL QUALITY
Good
ROUND TRIP
<0.1 mile
THE EXPERIENCE
★

Walk from the parking lot to the nearby Superior Street Bridge and look downstream to see Japp Hole Waterfall. For reasons we don't know, part of the falls is redirected by a thick concrete wall, forcing the river to hug the rocky bank, dropping here and there before emptying into a very large and deep pool beneath the railroad trestle. This pool is named the "Japp Hole." We were told the Japp family were the original owners of a greenhouse that still overlooks the falls here.

Gunderson's Falls

Between the Japp Hole and the stone bridge by the Lester Park parking lot is a small waterfall known to locals as Gunderson's Waterfall, named for a man who operated a nearby hamburger stand many years ago. This modest waterfall drops about 4 feet over a large rock shelf. Many families and teenagers gather on the rocks to swim in the slow water below the falls.

HIKE DIFFICULTY
Easy
TRAIL QUALITY
Good
ROUND TRIP
<0.1 mile
THE EXPERIENCE
★

While Lester River *was named by white settlers after an early land claimant, the Ojibwe called it Busabika-ziba—"River that comes through a Worn Hollow Place in the Rock."*

The Shallows or Lester Falls

HIKE DIFFICULTY
Moderate

TRAIL QUALITY
Fair

ROUND TRIP
0.2 mile

THE EXPERIENCE
★ ★ ★

TRAILHEAD: From Superior Street, go north on Lester River Road about 0.4 mile and park along the left where a gravel path heads towards the river.

Follow the gravel path a short way to the crest of Lester Falls. (You can view the falls from vantage points above the river that are bound by the cable railings.) It is a short walk down river to a steep flight of 28 tall stone steps leading to the river's edge. The steps lead to a path with slightly precarious footing. The falls, very audible, are soon visible. About 20 feet tall, the water pours down a craggy rock face. Below the falls is a large, shallow pool where you may see folks fishing or wading.

Nude Swimming Hole Falls

HIKE DIFFICULTY
Moderate

TRAIL QUALITY
Good to Poor

ROUND TRIP
0.6 mile

THE EXPERIENCE
★ ★ ★

TRAILHEAD: From Superior Street, drive 1.2 miles up river on Lester Road. Park in a small gravel turn-out on your left. You'll hear the river when you get out. A wide gravel path, which looks like an old road, heads down river to Nude Swimming Hole Waterfall. Note: You may want to visit this risqué waterfall when the weather is chilly.

Before heading down the gravel road to Nude Swimming Hole Waterfall, look immediately to the right, where a small path leads to an overlook of a three-tiered waterfall rounding a tight corner. Head downriver on the gravel road. Within a few minutes, you will hear another waterfall below. A very short spur path leads to a view of a gentle, 6-foot high waterfall that empties, in two steps, into a large pool. Two minutes farther along the gravel road, another small slide foams over craggy rocks.

Three minutes more and the gravel road transitions to grass. At this point, a dirt path heads sharply right toward the river. Follow this to the river's edge and head downriver. You will soon see an 8-foot waterfall that is just above the Nude

Swimming Hole Waterfall. The path climbs a steep incline. After cresting the rise, look right to see the top of Nude Swimming Hole Waterfall. The impressive fall spills over a wide shelf of gray rock, fanning out as it drops about 10 feet. Broad outcroppings beside the fall are great for contemplation and a close-up view. We saw numerous stone cairns around the edge of the Nude Swimming Hole pool. Return time from this mystical setting to the trailhead: eight minutes.

The Nude Swimming Hole Falls

Two Sisters Falls

TRAILHEAD: From Superior Street, take Lester River Road up river 1.3 miles. Park in a small, gravel turnout on your left. A short, dirt trail leads to the waterfall.

This stepped, 10-foot waterfall is made up of two, side-by-side falls occurring on the bottom curve of an S in the river. The left slide is longer and larger than its "sister" on the right. (Note: This name is totally our own.) Along the river is a pleasant grassy area where rock outcroppings create comfortable, informal seating.

HIKE DIFFICULTY
Easy
TRAIL QUALITY
Good
ROUND TRIP
<0.1 mile
THE EXPERIENCE
★ ★

French River Falls above the Expressway

FRENCH RIVER
Northeast of Duluth

French River Falls

TRAILHEAD: As you leave Duluth, the Highway 61 Expressway curves left and Scenic Highway 61 stays near the shore. The French River is 6.4 miles up Scenic Highway 61. Park in a small lot on the lake side of the highway at the river. Across the highway is a Minnesota Department of Natural Resources fish hatchery. Cross on the highway bridge to the west side of the river, where you will see a dirt trail.

HIKE DIFFICULTY
Moderate
TRAIL QUALITY
Poor to Fair
ROUND TRIP
0.7 mile
THE EXPERIENCE
★ to ★★★

Walking up the west bank, you will first pass the concrete fish ladder and observation chutes. Just upriver is a series of small cascades a few feet high and man-made steps for the fish to ascend the falls. The root-strewn path, covered with red pine needles, winds its way back and forth through balsams and ferns, ill-defined in places. About five minutes from the bridge, the path seems to peter out as you walk on rocks near a small waterfall. The path picks up again higher up the bank and takes you past a large dam and metal grate. Seagulls may be swirling overhead. Look for blue-bead lily at your feet. Five minutes beyond this, you will see a 50-yard series of 2- to 5-foot cascades spilling and tumbling over the gentle slope of gray, volcanic rock leading beyond the railroad trestle suspended high above the river. There are nice spots for reflective thought where you can sit beside the cascade.

Angwassago-zibi —"Floodwater River" was the Ojibwe name for the French River, *highly appropriate given the river's sensitivity to seasonal flow. "Rivière des Français" followed, which was then translated to its present moniker.*

French River

French River Falls
North of the Expressway

TRAILHEAD: If you are on the Highway 61 Expressway, turn north onto County Road 50, also called Ryan Road, which is just west of the French River. Pull over and park on the shoulder of Ryan Road. Walk back to the ditch of the expressway and follow it east, 100 yards, to the French River.

HIKE DIFFICULTY
Easy
TRAIL QUALITY
Fair
ROUND TRIP
< 0.2 mile
THE EXPERIENCE
★★★★

The French River waterfalls north of the expressway are the real deal. To see these impressive falls, stand on the ditch bank below the expressway guardrail directly above the river where it passes under the highway. Unless you come this far, you can only see the bottom of the waterfall. From here, though, you see most of it as it carves its way through gray rock, surrounded by white pine, cedar and balsam. There is an upper section, difficult to see, with about a 6-foot drop. The middle section has a 15-foot drop, where the river is wider, lacier, and tumbles over a ledge in several places before forming a long, narrow pool. The bottom section is a thin, 15-foot waterfall that hugs a high canyon wall, its ledges draped in rust-colored blankets of white pine needles.

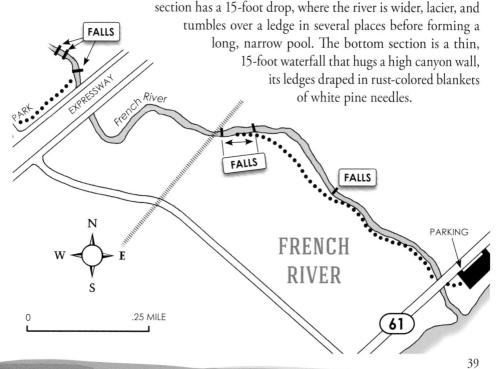

Waterfall by bridge spanning Schmidt Creek

SCHMIDT CREEK
Northeast of Duluth

Schmidt Creek Falls

TRAILHEAD: At about mile marker 12 on the Highway 61 Expressway, turn inland on County Road 50, also called Ryan Road. In about two blocks, Ryan Road takes a 90-degree right turn. You will first cross over the French River. A half-mile from Highway 61, turn right on Old North Shore Road. Take this dirt road 0.4 mile to its dead end at large red and white barriers.

HIKE DIFFICULTY
Easy
TRAIL QUALITY
Good
ROUND TRIP
< 0.1 mile
THE EXPERIENCE
★ ★

Walk past the barriers on the old roadway. About 50 feet farther you will come to an old bridge spanning Schmidt Creek. Look upstream and see a picturesque waterfall nestled in a little valley heavily wooded with cedars and aspens. It is surprising how quiet it is here, just a short way from the expressway. The first time we visited, a deer was drinking in the creek just above the waterfall. The creek spills in two steps, for a total of about 6 feet, and then continues in a long slide that passes directly under the bridge.

The average depth of Lake Superior *is 489 feet, with a maximum depth of 1333 feet. It takes 400-500 years for a complete water change.*

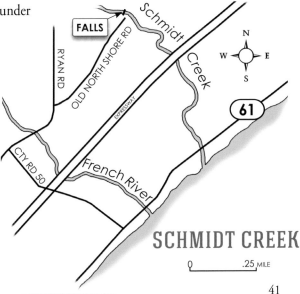

SCHMIDT CREEK

0 .25 MILE

Sucker River Falls

SUCKER RIVER
Northeast of Duluth

Sucker River Falls

TRAILHEAD: From Duluth, take Scenic Highway 61 9.2 miles to the Sucker River. The parking area is on the lake side, with a line of spruce marking the edge of the lot, and a "Minnesota Lake Superior Coastal Program" sign. A steep trail leads down to the river at the west end of the lot, taking you to a minor waterfall. The good stuff, though, is found above the bridge.

HIKE DIFFICULTY
Moderate
TRAIL QUALITY
Poor
ROUND TRIP
0.5 mile
THE EXPERIENCE
★ to ★★★

The Sucker River was first named for its spring sucker run. The stretch between Scenic Highway 61 and the expressway is now a popular place to fish for trout. For us, the abundance and beauty of its waterfalls was a pleasant surprise.

Directly across the highway from the parking lot, a well-worn path leads down to the east bank of the river. It will take you under the railroad trestle and by a small step of waterfall/rapids. There is a dirt path along the edge of the river and another higher up on the bank, which may be preferable when the water is running high. The river soon takes a 90-degree turn to the left. At river's edge, you'll find a 5-foot rock that you have to slide down in order to continue upstream. On the return trip, you may require a boost from behind by a more athletic hiking partner in order to get over it. It's worth the extra effort, as once you round that corner you are treated to a beautiful 5-foot waterfall. From the river's edge, you will have a unique perspective of the falls directly in front of you, with the portion of the river above the falls, just at eye level, that seems as motionless as glass. Walk a short distance up the river, and you can enjoy a perch on the rocks in the midst of this watery display.

Follow the east side of the river for roughly another 50 yards, climbing over and around rocks and going around another bend, to encounter another small cascade.

The Ojibwe name "Namebini-zibi" survived translation as the "Sucker River," *named for the type of fish inhabiting this river. It was also, at one time, known as "Carp River."*

Just before the next waterfall, the trail skirts up and around, winding beneath lovely cedar trees, serpent-like roots complicating (and complementing) your way. There are some rough, rocky stretches, as well, though upon closer inspection, even these pesky rocks are adorned with lovely pink speckles. At this point, you can hear the rumble of something significant ahead and your anticipation builds. The trail winds beneath cedar and balsam just 20 feet from the river's edge. About 100 yards upstream from the previous waterfall, you find the best falls on the Sucker River: a gorgeous,

Altered three-tiered waterfall on the Sucker River

12-foot, three-tiered cascade. Columbine and old cedars grace the watery, rocky scene, with a convenient rock spit located in front of the show, allowing a head-on perspective of the waterfall. Interestingly, this is an example of an "altered" waterfall. Jackhammers, drills and dynamite were artfully employed at one time, by the DNR, to sculpt these cascades and aid fish in their passage upstream. After being "wowed" by this waterfall, if you want to continue upriver, you will encounter two more minor falls and then reach the culvert beneath the expressway, perhaps 40 minutes from when your hike began. For us, the round trip up and back lasted approximately one hour.

The French, Sucker, Talmadge, *and* Knife rivers *tantalized early settlers with small and scattered finds of copper, feeding dreams of larger deposits similar to those found on the Keweenaw Peninsula of Upper Michigan. Though prospecting flourished in the area in the mid and late 1800s, and several mining operations were established, yields were never large enough to be profitable.*

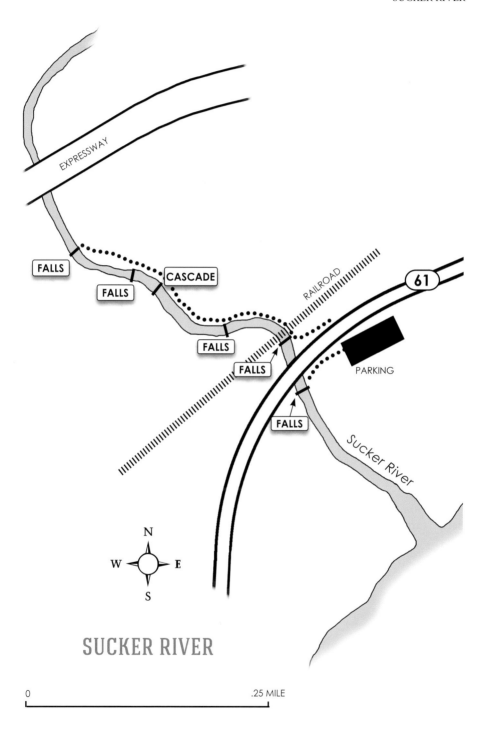

SUCKER RIVER

0   .25 MILE

Second Falls on the Knife River

KNIFE RIVER
Knife River

First Falls

TRAILHEAD: The Knife River falls are most easily accessed from the wayside rest/historical marker located at mile marker 18 on the Highway 61 Expressway, 13 miles northeast of Duluth. At the far west side of the parking lot there is a blacktop path that quickly turns into gravel and descends down a small bank to the river.

HIKE DIFFICULTY
Moderate
TRAIL QUALITY
Fair to Good
ROUND TRIP
0.2 mile
THE EXPERIENCE
★

From the wayside rest, you can walk to First Falls in about a minute. The path comes out below the First Falls, on a large, red rock outcropping. The river splits and drops several times in a series of falls ranging from 2 to 8 feet. On the west side of the river, is a fish ladder and weir constructed to capture steelhead trout for study as they make their way upstream to spawning areas. When the water is low, you can walk across the rocks to the fish ladder. At high flow, you have to walk across the expressway bridge to reach the other side. In the spring, you may see large steelhead jumping up the falls and many anglers in the stream below. The falls area is closed to fishing.

Second Falls

TRAILHEAD: From the Highway 61 Expressway, turn north on Shilhon Road at about mile marker 18. A sign says "No Outlet." Take this gravel road 0.7 mile to its end. There is a small parking area on the right, just before the turn-around. You will see a trail marked by a brown DNR sign outlining trout fishing regulations.

HIKE DIFFICULTY
Moderate
TRAIL QUALITY
Good
ROUND TRIP
1.25 miles
THE EXPERIENCE
★ ★ ★

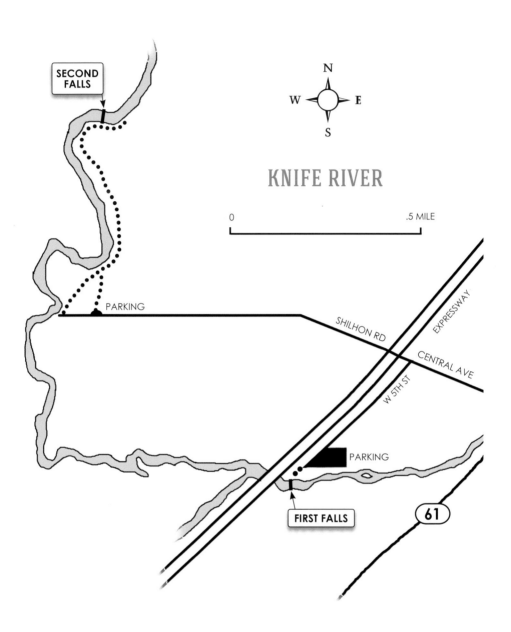

SECOND
FALLS

KNIFE RIVER

0   .5 MILE

PARKING

SHILHON RD

EXPRESSWAY

CENTRAL AVE

W 5TH ST

PARKING

FIRST FALLS

61

At the trailhead to Second Falls, a pastel sign reads: Knife River Hiking Trail. The way starts out grassy, but soon transitions to a well-worn dirt path. We rated the hike difficulty as moderate only because of the distance and one stretch of steps. Otherwise the going is easy.

At the time of this writing, the path that runs closest to the river was blocked off, and we were diverted to the right. After a few minutes, you'll see a path going left, back into the trees, but instead go straight ahead along the grassy edge of the woods. Eventually, the trail goes back into the woods and brings you alongside the river. You will see a narrow, steep path that heads down to the river onto a basalt outcropping beside a small waterfall—not Second Falls, yet. Red pines across the river and cedars overhead make for a pleasant place to watch the falls split around a low table of rock.

Back on the main trail, continue upriver. In a minute, you'll see a sign reading, "Superior Hiking Trail, Second Falls—.5 mile." Make your way along the needle-carpeted path. After crossing two wooden bridges spanning small creek beds, the path forks. Stay right and go up a slight rise along a path lined with wire tree cages (it's well-known that after dark, the trees in this area go wild). You'll come to a stretch of 31 earthen steps, reinforced with moss-covered railroad ties. Not far past a sign indicating an old copper mining site on the right side of the trail, you'll see and hear the cascades below. A petite path winds down through the pines to the falls.

The Knife River splits around a large rock island, which serves as a catch basin for the large spines of once towering pines that wash downstream in high water. Notice the pile up of debris from the flood of 2012 along the shore. The water to the right of the island runs over a few steps to a last 4-foot drop. The left side is tantalizingly difficult to view. From your position on the jet-black, lichen-covered rocks, however, the right falls is more than satisfying. A quiet, backwater pool is tucked behind you, backed by a shallow cave arch crowned with conifers. This waterfall, though modest, occurs in such a pleasant environment and at the end of such an agreeable northwoods jaunt, that the experience earns our three-star rating. If you go a minute farther upriver, you'll find a path with a log banister to aid your way to other smaller falls.

The Ojibwe "Makomani-zibi" was translated to "Knife River," *so-called because of the sharp rocks lining the riverbed.*

Fifth Falls

GOOSEBERRY RIVER
Gooseberry State Park

Middle and Lower Falls

TRAILHEAD: Approaching from the west on Highway 61, turn right into the Gooseberry State Park campground and visitor center. Bear left to the visitor center parking lot. Even with ample parking, on weekends the park can be very busy, so you may have to be patient and drive around until you find an open spot. At the visitor center, grab a map of the park.

HIKE DIFFICULTY
Easy
TRAIL QUALITY
Good
ROUND TRIP
1 mile
THE EXPERIENCE
★★★ to ★★★★

Gooseberry Falls State Park is one of the North Shore's most popular attractions, due to the fabulous waterfalls within easy walking distance. Falls Loop Trail begins at the visitor center. After a short distance, the trail splits. Head right to the Middle and Lower Falls. (If you go left it will take you to the Plaza and Bridge Overlook.) At 0.1 mile, the trail splits again. Go right, take the few steps down, and shortly you will find yourself next to Middle Falls. Here the Gooseberry River begins a final 65-foot plunge before flowing out to Lake Superior. The wide, horseshoe-shaped Middle Falls drops 25 feet onto a large volcanic rock ledge where it then splits around a large rock outcropping to form the Lower Falls. Each half of the Lower Falls is unique. Both plunge 40 feet before the river rejoins.

As you follow Falls Loop Trail down the west side, there is easy access to the rocks at the base of both Middle and Lower Falls. Particularly at Middle Falls, if the water volume isn't too great, you can walk very near to the torrent. There may be many

---

Some say the Gooseberry River *may have been named after a 17th- century explorer whose name, "Groseilliers," means "gooseberry" in French. The Ojibwe name for this river was Shabonimikani-zibi or "Place of the Gooseberries." The gooseberry is a small indigenous bush found widely on the North Shore. The mouth of the Gooseberry River was a headquarters and launching point for huge volumes of timber brought in by rail from the area and then rafted to mills in Wisconsin and Michigan.*

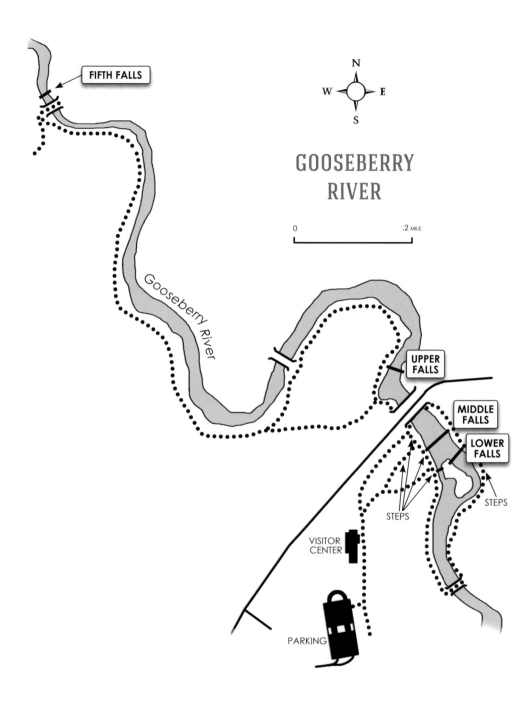

FIFTH FALLS

N
W E
S

GOOSEBERRY
RIVER

0 .2 MILE

Gooseberry River

UPPER
FALLS

MIDDLE
FALLS

LOWER
FALLS

STEPS

STEPS

VISITOR
CENTER

PARKING

Middle Falls

people here. One day when we visited, some East Indian women, dressed all in white, were singing in their native tongue by Lower Falls. The mist and their music swirled up into the heavens.

The Falls Loop Trail is well-maintained and relatively free of obstructions. Since it follows the river along the falls, there are some steps to negotiate, but they are well-constructed wooden steps. The trail takes you below Lower Falls, where it crosses east over the river on a footbridge. As you cross the bridge, be sure to look upstream for a fabulous panoramic view of both the Middle and Lower Falls. The return trail on the east side of the river rises quickly, giving you great views looking down on the river and both falls, especially Middle Falls.

Upper Falls

HIKE DIFFICULTY
Easy

TRAIL QUALITY
Good

ROUND TRIP
0.5 mile

THE EXPERIENCE
★ ★ ★ ★

Take the asphalt trail behind the visitor center. Stay to the left and take the Falls Loop Trail towards the Highway 61 bridge. Follow the large stone Plaza Wall on your left. The trail eventually crosses over the river on a footbridge beneath the Highway 61 bridge. From the footbridge, you can look upstream and see Upper Falls tumbling in twin cascades 30 feet into a swirling, white pool. Retrace your steps to the west end of the footbridge. You can go upriver on the trail, and soon be at an overlook opposite Upper Falls. Notice the caverns directly behind the overlook. If you follow the path farther along the river to the top of Upper Falls, you will have a beautiful view of Lake Superior in the distance, but be careful. You could walk to Upper Falls and back in about 20 to 30 minutes if you don't stop to sit and take in the scenery. But please do so.

Fifth Falls

HIKE DIFFICULTY
Moderate to
Strenuous

TRAIL QUALITY
Poor to Good

ROUND TRIP
1.8 miles

THE EXPERIENCE
★ ★ ★

To get to the Fifth Falls of Gooseberry River, begin at Upper Falls and follow the trail 0.7 mile upstream along the west side of the river. The trail is not as well maintained as the Loop Trail. There are some roots and sometimes mud. Smaller paths branch off the trail going to river overlooks. From Upper Falls, it takes about 12 minutes to reach a small footbridge crossing the river. Rather than crossing this bridge, however, continue on the west side of the river on the Fifth Falls Trail. In a few more minutes, you'll see a map and sign that reads: Fifth Falls Snowshoe Trail. The trail splits here. Stay to the right along the river.

Fewer people take the time to walk to Fifth Falls, so it is a much quieter experience than the other falls at Gooseberry. You may see Turks cap lilies, bunchberry, and bluebead lilies along the way. Following the river, you'll pass some small cascades. The trail is narrower and a little more strenuous than the Loop Trail, but a

Upper Falls

half-hour hike leads to your reward. Just before you reach Fifth Falls, you'll find a trail shelter. Look across the river to see grottos at the base of the canyon walls, just above waterline. In another minute you're at the falls.

From a promontory you can see a series of small drops descending about 35 feet over chunks of basalt through the narrow gorge. The rock walls are pocketed with fern-lined grottos and draped in cedars. Cross the footbridge, hanging just above the falls, for a view downriver. Take Fifth Falls Trail down the east side of the river to some flat rocks along the falls—prime seating for the water show. On the east side, Fifth Falls Trail follows the same path as the Superior Hiking Trail. The footing is a little better, with wooden boardwalks in some places, and it takes you higher above the river. There are no guardrails, so beware of the steep drops down.

Look closely on the forest floor for goblet lichen *or "pixie cup." No more than 1 inch high, it resembles tiny, pale green wine glasses. It is often found among moss and other types of lichens.*

Nelsens Creek Falls

NELSENS CREEK
Gooseberry State Park

Nelsens Creek Falls

TRAILHEAD: Nelsens Creek is the next water body northeast of Gooseberry River, about 0.7 mile up the highway from the Gooseberry Park entrance. Be aware that there is no great place to park along the highway, however. We just pulled over on the shoulder.

HIKE DIFFICULTY
Easy to Strenuous
(depending on
water level and
how far you walk)
TRAIL QUALITY
Good to Poor
ROUND TRIP
<0.1 to 0.2 mile
THE EXPERIENCE
★ ★

You will see the falls right away as you look upstream from the highway. When the water is low, you can walk easily along the creek right up to the 15-foot rock face over which the creek gently spills. A large tree, fallen long ago, lies suspended across and just above the face of the waterfall. Since the water flows inconsistently in this creek, long strands of algae hang like banners on the steeper parts of the rock face. Pads of moss carpet the gentler slopes.

In spring, high water forced us to take a more circuitous route high up the bank on the left in order to see the upper part of the falls. The upper part of this falls is actually more interesting than the more readily observable lower portion, though not as large. Before Nelsens Creek takes the lower plunge, it falls down a 6-foot sloping ledge, fanning out as it slides. It empties into a small pool and then takes a hard right in order to get around a large rock outcropping. The fall and abrupt change in direction create a lot of suds so that the pool, when we were there, was covered in glistening white foam. There are several flat rocks to sit on, right at the edge of this intimate pool. Get comfortable and enjoy the view.

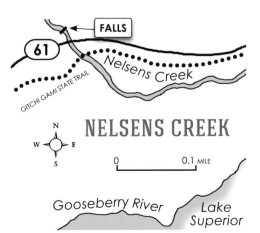

West Branch Falls

Split Rock River
Split Rock Lighthouse State Park

Split Rock River Falls

TRAILHEAD: Park in the Highway 61 wayside, near mile marker 46, on the west bank of the Split Rock River. The trailhead begins from the parking lot and is well marked.

HIKE DIFFICULTY
Moderate to Strenuous

TRAIL QUALITY
Good to Poor

DISTANCE
1 mile to West Branch Split Rock River Falls. 4.1 miles to the final falls

THE EXPERIENCE
★★★ to ★★★★

The scenic lighthouse and splendid views of Lake Superior are just a portion of what this state park offers. We counted nine major waterfalls in 1.3 miles, one of the most impressive stretches of north country rivers we've seen. You won't find any of the Split Rock River waterfalls marked on the official state park map, but be assured they are there in abundance. By our estimation, the Split Rock River is the most prolific North Shore river for waterfalls. Though this is not a short hike, you may actually begin to feel spoiled, as you see waterfall after waterfall and begin to say things like, "There's another one?" Due to steep river banks, some of the falls are only visible from high above the river through heavy forest cover, so we recommend this hike before the trees leaf out—in the spring (lasting through most of May) or in the autumn.

An interpretive sign near the beginning of the path explains the Ojibwe name for this river is Gin-On-Wab-Iko-Zibi or Eagle-Iron-River. Near the highway, the river appears deceptively placid. A well-maintained trail passes through birch and conifers, with few roots or rocks to step over. About a half-mile into the hike, go right where you see a sign saying, "Split Rock River Crossing 1.8 miles." Fifty-five steps take you down to a shaded elfin glen contained by rock walls covered in moss and lichen. To your left you will see a footbridge traversing a side-creek, called West

---

The Split Rock River *is named after two cliffs one mile east of the mouth, which appear to be split apart. Logging was heavy here at the turn of the century. Split Rock Lumber Company built railroad lines to a dammed pond at the river's mouth; from there rafts of logs were towed by tugs to Duluth.*

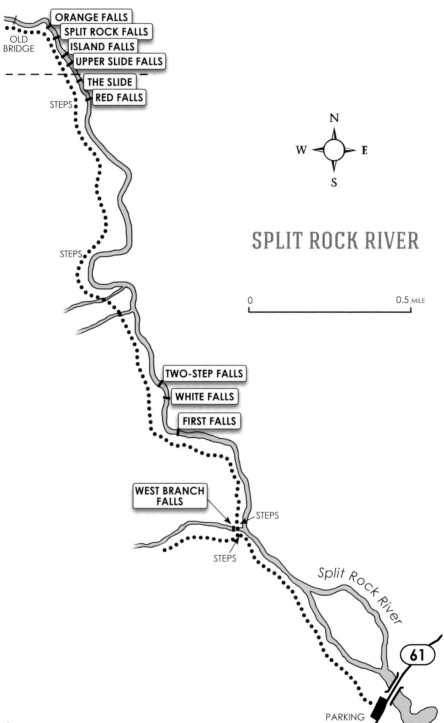

ORANGE FALLS
SPLIT ROCK FALLS
ISLAND FALLS
UPPER SLIDE FALLS
THE SLIDE
RED FALLS

OLD BRIDGE

STEPS

STEPS

STEPS

N
W   E
S

SPLIT ROCK RIVER

0   0.5 MILE

TWO-STEP FALLS
WHITE FALLS
FIRST FALLS

WEST BRANCH FALLS

STEPS

STEPS

Split Rock River

61

PARKING

Branch Split Rock River. From this bridge, behold a glistening waterfall cascading about 20 feet into a serene pool. Sunlight filters through the trees and illuminates the clear water. A small spur path going left, just across the bridge, continues a few yards to a bench that presents an up-close and personal waterfall experience.

White Falls

Pick up the main trail again and climb 32 steps beyond the bridge, where the trail curves and ascends to the right. You are now on the Superior Hiking Trail. You will begin hearing the Split Rock River ahead. The quality of the trail, from this point on, is fair to poor, with some steep stretches. About 20 minutes into the hike, you will overlook the first falls on the Split Rock River, about a quarter mile beyond the West Branch Falls.

Unfortunately, there is no clear view of this cascade, due to the trees. You will catch tantalizing glimpses of red rock and white water rushing down a chute that widens near the bottom. "First Falls," as we refer to it, swings around a tight turn as it drops 20 feet between white lichen-encrusted walls. Perhaps the fact that you can't quite see it all adds to its allure, like cleavage. Others, eager to see the falls up close, have sought a way down the seeming suicidal slopes, adding to a serious erosion problem. (In our humble opinion, the state should invest in some stairs down this slope and stabilize the bank.) First Falls embodies the character shared by all the falls along the Split Rock River: Cedars cling tenaciously to rosy-red cliffs, and highly fractured rocks render water a brilliant white as it skids down slides in a seemingly unending procession.

Continuing up the trail, you will encounter a stretch of well-constructed boardwalks and railroad-tie steps, making your trek a bit easier. About five minutes beyond First Falls, you will round a bend and see in the distance what we refer to as "White Falls," a gradual, lacy slide that drops about 30 feet. You can view it from a rock outcropping about 50 yards downriver from the base of the falls. With a larger drop than First Falls, it also has a wider slope and occurs over a shorter span, making it more dramatic.

A stone's throw upriver from White Falls is a minor slide. About two minutes of walking brings you to the third major fall, which we refer to as "Two-Step." Again, there isn't a good view of these falls from the bank nor a good way to get down to river level. Looking from a distance, the river winds towards you as it completes a large S-turn. At the upper turn of the S, the river splits around a rock outcrop, forming two lacy falls of 10 to 15 feet. At the lower turn of the S, it narrows and drops again in a smaller, single waterfall. From here, the trail rises and the pleasant hike continues over a small bridge spanning a creek. You have moved away from Split Rock River proper and will hike along the tributary creek, cross another bridge, climb 20 steps up, some down, and negotiate some roots. About one minute past the second bridge, you begin to descend and hear the Split Rock River again. It is pretty rough going at this point and the trail quality is poor. The river and trail snake along, and you pass several rapids before reaching the fourth falls, about 15 minutes after Two-Step. The path leads right out on a rock outcrop beside the waterfall.

We refer to this fourth major falls as "Red Falls." It runs for approximately 100 feet, gradually dropping about 30 feet, hugging the rock wall beneath you as it curves along the riverbed before emptying into an enormous pool. Our name comes from the red rock forming the shelf the water spills over and the striking, lichen-covered canyon wall on the opposite side of the river. This is a good place to sit and rest.

Moving on, five minutes upriver, and after climbing up precarious red rocks and 28 railroad tie steps, you look down on a graceful fifth waterfall, "The Slide." The river is broad here and the waterfall spreads itself thin across the whole width as it gently caresses the many rock shelves, while concentrating most of its efforts to the far left. Two minutes later, after passing a sign reading, "Leaving Split Rock State Park," you encounter the sixth waterfall, which we call "The Upper Slide." As you stand beside the falls, the river turns to the right, carving gray and red canyon walls speckled with lichen and topped off with conifers. The water is stirred white as it passes over fractured rock faces. The gentle falls spread across the whole riverbed, and you can get closer to this cascade than any of the others you've passed. Below the falls, the river runs wide and shallow on bedrock shelves.

Another minute of walking leads to the seventh falls, which you can see from a promontory to the right of the trail. Looking upriver, you will see a tall rock island where several conifers grow. The divided river falls around both sides of the rocks. The right side is usually a trickle, while the left is a vigorous two-stepped chute. We refer to this as Island Falls.

The path continues up and then down stone steps. About 50 feet beyond the bottom, you will see an unusual geological phenomenon: a stately pair of 15- to 20-foot rock spires standing side by side. Looking through the opening between the spires, you can see the eighth major waterfall, a series of large, gradual steps leading the river around a bend. High red cliffs tower over the far side of the river, topped with evergreens that occasionally reach down to water's edge. The trail crosses a stretch of brick-red rock shards, which clatter beneath your feet like falling bowling pins. Two minutes later, you reach the ninth falls. A fitting finale to this riotous river, we call it "Orange Falls" because of the vibrant orange lichen just above

Red Falls

river level on the rock walls across the river. Water slides and drops 20 feet in long troughs along two sides of a fractured rock outcropping. Look for sponge-like reindeer lichen growing along the trail.

You can turn back here, and cut a half mile of additional hiking from your trek, or you can go on to the next river crossing. Beyond the bridge crossing, the trail follows the other side of the river for about a half mile before heading east in a long, circuitous route to Highway 61, ending up 0.35 mile east of the trailhead. We headed back the way we came from Orange Falls and it took us about an hour to make the return trip—45 minutes to the West Branch Falls bridge, and 10 minutes more to the parking lot.

Lichens *are non-flowering plants occurring in many forms and colors, which you can see growing in deep moist forest, as well as on dry rock outcroppings along the North Shore and its rivers. They grow where there is little competition from other plants – such as on rocks, tree trunks, and fallen logs.*

Beaver River Falls

BEAVER RIVER

Beaver Bay

Beaver River Falls

TRAILHEAD: The Beaver River borders the east edge of "downtown" Beaver Bay. You can view falls from the Highway 61 bridge or by walking down to the river. Park at the lot at the intersection of Lax Lake Road and Highway 61, just west of the Beaver River bridge, where people park for the Gitchi Gami Trail.

HIKE DIFFICULTY
Easy to bridge/
Moderate to river

TRAIL QUALITY
Good to bridge/
Poor to river

DISTANCE ROUND TRIP
0.25 mile to falls

THE EXPERIENCE
★★★★ to
★★★★★

Most people only get a glimpse of the Beaver River Falls from the periphery of their vision while driving over the Highway 61 bridge. This is a shame because the waterfalls deserve a good, long look. A walkway along the bridge provides a panoramic eagle's eye view of four tumbling torrents, just above the highway. The cascades roar as clouds of mist roll up from the river.

For a more intimate waterfall experience, walk down to the river's edge. Start from the parking area at the intersection of Lax Lake Road and Highway 61. Two dirt paths head toward the river. Don't take the one on the right that goes under a power line near the bridge. The path you want starts from the middle of the parking area and immediately forks. Take the left fork, which goes steeply down the bank into a ravine. The quality of the path here is poor. At the bottom of the ravine, you will cross a small brook. Continue on, and in about three minutes you will be at the river's edge. You can go right, to the falls nearest the bridge, or go left, to the two upper falls.

Going toward the bridge, several paths lead through the brush and trees, and over rocks and boulders to the falls. Be careful. This lower waterfall is actually two falls, where the river splits and tumbles around an outcropping and big, black boulders, dropping about 20 to 25 feet.

The Beaver River *was named after the many beaver colonies found at one time along its length.*

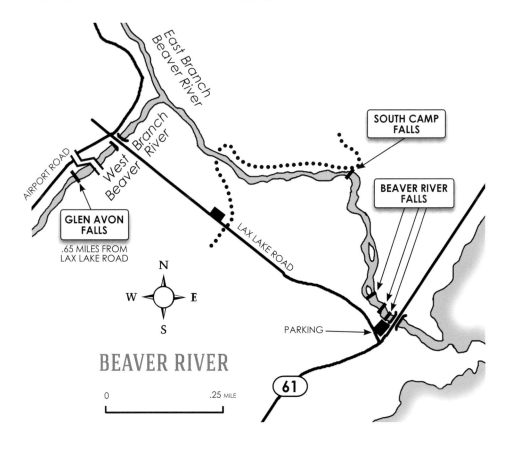

East Branch
Beaver River

West Branch
Beaver River

AIRPORT ROAD

GLEN AVON FALLS

.65 MILES FROM
LAX LAKE ROAD

SOUTH CAMP FALLS

BEAVER RIVER FALLS

LAX LAKE ROAD

PARKING

N
W · E
S

BEAVER RIVER

0   .25 MILE

61

Going left, a short path brings you to the middle falls. Slicing through a narrow, 4-foot wide slot in a broad rock face, the river falls about 25 feet. Look for a rainbow suspended just above the turbulent falls.

Continuing upriver, the trail is relatively easy. It takes you over bedrock as smooth as pavement. In two minutes you reach the base of the third falls, the smallest of the three, but no less distinctive. Walk under the cedars clinging to the rocks at the river's edge to stand on the rock ledges beside the waterfall. A forested island divides the waterfalls. Closest to you is a 10- to 15-foot drop. This is the upper waterfall visible from the bridge. Near the base of the falls are some potholes—1 to 3 feet in diameter—ground into the rock by the incessant swirling of sand and water. Beyond

The peculiar puffball *fungi may appear as a cluster of beige spheres, about 1 to 2 inches in diameter, with a small hole on top of each one. If you nudge one, spores will come puffing out of the hole.*

the island is another waterfall comprised of several steps over which the water flows. This is not visible from the Highway 61 bridge and was a pleasant surprise for us the first time we saw it.

South Camp Falls

TRAILHEAD: From Highway 61 in Beaver Bay, turn north on Lax Lake Road (Lake County Road 4) and proceed 0.8 mile. On your right, you will see a parking area for the Superior Hiking Trail, near some large holding ponds. Park here. The trail to the falls begins as a wide gravel road.

HIKE DIFFICULTY
Moderate
TRAIL QUALITY
Fair
ROUND TRIP
2 miles
THE EXPERIENCE
★ ★ ★

After passing the ponds, the road bends right and within seven minutes comes to a small suspension bridge. As soon as you cross the bridge, look for a sign marking the Superior Hiking Trail, which follows the Beaver River. This hike is full of natural splendors—stately conifers and rugged rocks set with tablecloths of ferns. The path passes a campsite, denoted by a sign saying North Beaver River. The river begins gathering speed near a small log bridge at a muddy spot in the trail. The path rises above the river, and then heads back down. A rapids begins near the South Beaver River campsite leading to the waterfall just downstream, hence our name for the falls.

Constrained in a 20-foot downward plunge by volcanic rock, the river has carved a stepped, serpentine channel.

South Camp Falls

Once-sharp rock edges look recently smoothed, and seem arranged as main floor, front-row seating to observe the battling elements. One seat beside the rushing water even sports a backrest. See if you can find it. We left South Camp Falls reluctantly. This section of the Beaver River is a north country paradise. Our return hike took 22 minutes.

Glen Avon Falls

HIKE DIFFICULTY	
Easy	
TRAIL QUALITY	
Good	
DISTANCE	
ROUND TRIP	
0.25 mile	
THE EXPERIENCE	
★ ★ ★	

TRAILHEAD: Just west of the Beaver River bridge, Lax Lake Road (County Road 4) intersects with Highway 61. Head north 1.6 miles on Lax Lake Road, then turn left on County Road 3. Follow County Road 3 for 1.2 miles, where you will see a narrow, red dirt road heading left toward the river.

Glen Avon Falls is a gem—an Elizabeth Taylor-sized gem—little-known to the casual North Shore traveler, but apparently well-known to local folks and yellow swallow-tail butterflies. Park and walk about 40 yards across exposed red rock outcrop to the river's edge. The Beaver River saunters placidly along to this juncture, only to widen into a climactic drop over an awesome run of over 100 tumbling yards, down and down over broad rock shelves. The river then narrows, lingering in a slow-drifting whirlpool before continuing on its way. The vista is picture-postcard perfect, set in a broad valley with a distant emerald ridge shielding Superior from view and adding dramatic background and depth.

This area offers a great opportunity to explore. Head left on a dirt (sometimes mud) path to go a bit farther downriver and reach the wide rock terraces. Looking upriver, you will see that a 50-foot wide section of the river is caught up by a horizontal rock ridge, marked by a mysterious 3-foot notch in the rock bank across the river, just at water level. The ridge channels the flow perpendicular to the prevailing current until it is released, again at a right angle, through a 6-foot wide passage, after which it again splays wide, then splits around a craggy island.

This waterfall is the centerpiece of a mystical, terraced domain, populated with twisted old cedar trees. See if you can spot the lichen-encrusted queue of them, guarding a rock throne shaded with three types of conifers. A natural series of steps

Glen Avon Falls

leads up from a small back water pool (look close to see the white quartz line crossing the floor of the pool) to the dais, which is flanked by an ancient cedar, standing on its aged pinched roots, while it leans upon a younger, straighter tree for support—the old guard watching over the young. Look also for secret side-falls—places where rivulets have found a way through the fractured rock formations.

The Cascades

BAPTISM RIVER
Tettegouche State Park

The Cascades

TRAILHEAD: Tettegouche State Park is located 4.5 miles northeast of Silver Bay on Highway 61. Turn in at the park entrance and take an immediate right. Drive past the park visitor center on the road to the campground and trailhead. Cross the Baptism River on the wooden bridge, and park in the lot on your left where the sign says Center Parking. Walk back on the road toward the river. On the left, where the guardrail ends, you'll see a sign reading Brook Trout Regulations. This is the trail to The Cascades.

HIKE DIFFICULTY
Moderate
TRAIL QUALITY
Good
ROUND TRIP
1.8 miles
THE EXPERIENCE
★★★★

Shortly after you start down the path, the trail divides. Go to the left, upstream. The trail winds through birches and occasional conifers along the river's shore. Wild strawberries hide among rocks covered in cushiony moss. Ferns carpet the forest floor. Bordered with logs in many places, the well-maintained path is easy to walk. Several angler paths with steps lead to the river.

After five minutes on the trail, you'll hear the river tumbling over and around huge rocks. Another few minutes of walking brings you to an overlook where the river splits into two channels. About 15 or 20 minutes into your hike there are about 60 steps leading down to the river, where you'll come out on a flat rock ledge below the falls. Yarrow, blue harebell, and wild roses grow in the cracks of the rock, making this a festive place to sit and take in The Cascades. The falls seem to come out of nowhere as the river drops 12 feet, like a natural waterslide. Sitting at water level provides an inspiring view of one of our favorite waterfalls. Rushing whitewater drowns out every other sound. Sit awhile and enjoy its music.

The delicate appearance of the small lavender bell-shaped flower, harebell *(also called bluebell), belies its toughness. They seem too dainty to thrive on the sun-baked rock outcrops where you often find them. Yet they do, seemingly impervious to the harsh growing environment they often share with the ever-present lichens.*

High Falls & Two Step Falls

HIKE DIFFICULTY
Strenuous

TRAIL QUALITY
Good

ROUND TRIP
1.4 miles to High
Falls from Trailhead
Parking, 1.9 miles
to High Falls and
Two Step Falls from
Trailhead Parking

THE EXPERIENCE
High Falls ★ ★ ★ ★
Two Step Falls ★ ★ ★

TRAILHEAD: Follow the campground road across the river on the wooden bridge. Continue past Center Parking to the trailhead parking lot, where a sign marks the start of High Falls Trail. The trailhead is across from campsite #19. **Note:** *Add 1.5 miles to these distances if you park in the State Rest Area.*

The 70-foot High Falls of the Baptism River has the geographical distinction of being the highest waterfall in Minnesota. Along the Canadian border, High Falls of the Pigeon River is higher but, technically, half of it is in Ontario. Whatever, both are majestic cascades. The Baptism's High Falls Trail rises sharply at first and soon intersects the Superior Hiking Trail. Go right, following a very wide and well-groomed path with few roots or rocks, although it is steep and strenuous in spots. The trail goes up the west side of the river, passing through a birch forest with a fairly open canopy. Bunchberries and thimbleberries decorate the forest floor. After about 15 minutes of walking, you'll find yourself at a wooden platform overlook of the High Falls. To your left, 67 wooden steps lead down to another observation platform, where the view is somewhat obscured by vegetation. Continue down 49 more steps for a better overview at the river bridge.

Cross the river on the springy suspension bridge just above the falls and head downstream. Please note that the bridge's walkway is a grate with large, open holes. Only bring a dog if

The High Falls

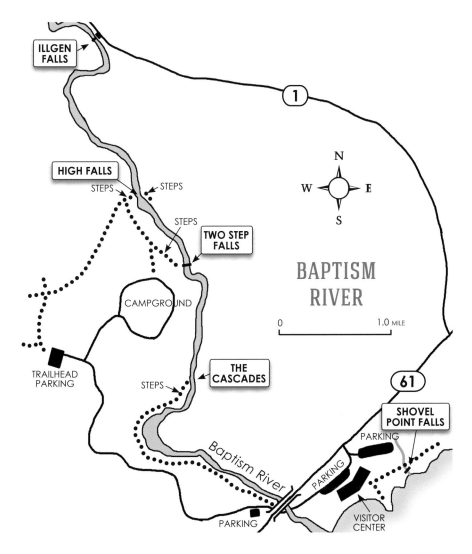

you're prepared to carry it across. A series of boardwalks and short runs of steps goes up and down…and up and down…leading to varied views of the falls. One hundred and fifty-seven wooden steps take you down to the river. Looking up, High Falls lunges out over the edge of the precipice, landing in a large, shallow pool. Mist dances high into the air, like spirits trying to reach the upper bluffs. Awesome!

The suspension bridge is the only hiking bridge that crosses the river, so to return to the trailhead or to continue to Two Step Falls, you have to climb up all of the steps you just descended. After you have gone back across the suspension bridge and reached the top of the steps, you can go right and return to the trailhead or go left to Two Step Falls and the campground.

Heading toward Two Step Falls, you will come to a fork in the path and a sign that says "1/8 mile to Two Step Falls, 1/2 mile back to High Falls." Take the left fork and proceed to the falls down a total of 175 stairs. The tiered falls first drop about 12 feet. Split by a large rock, the river tumbles into a pool, narrows, and breaks in two again for a second and smaller drop. The killer steps (especially following the trek to High Falls) definitely detract from the overall experience of Two Step Falls (or should it be called 175 Step Falls?). The climb back up is quite strenuous. When you get back to the sign indicating the distance to the Two Step and High Falls, go left to the campground. Walk through the campground on the road or take the path bisecting the campground, either way ending up at the restroom/shower building. Follow the road out of the campground, and when it splits, go right to the trailhead parking lot and your car.

Shovel Point Falls

HIKE DIFFICULTY
Moderate
TRAIL QUALITY
Good
ROUND TRIP
0.4 mile
THE EXPERIENCE
★ ★

TRAILHEAD: The trail to Shovel Point Falls begins from the parking area of the Tettegouche State Park Visitor Center. Go to the far-left parking lot. From the lake side of the parking lot, a paved trail angles toward the lake and leads to an overlook. The Shovel Point trail continues from the left side of the overlook.

This little waterfall is very easy to miss, but worthy of your special attention. It is located on a tiny creek that only exists if there has been ample rain in Tettegouche State Park. The Shovel Point Trail is one of our favorite North Shore hikes, with breathtaking views of Superior's untamed shores.

The walking distance to this waterfall is short, but includes 54 steps. The first steps descend to a small footbridge over an unnamed creek coming down the hillside. As soon as the creek passes beneath the bridge, it dives off a cliff edge, plummeting about 25 feet to the rocks and icy waters of Lake Superior below. You can't see much of the fall from the bridge, but a few steps beyond the bridge you'll find a path with a few more steps (whew!) down to an overlook with a bench. When there are no leaves on the trees, you can see this little gem plunging down the lichen-encrusted rock face. If you look west, in the distance you'll see the remnants of a mystic rock archway and mighty Palisade Head. Mood music is provided by the mellow sounds of the waterfall meeting the waves.

Illgen Falls

TRAILHEAD: The fourth falls on the Baptism River, Illgen Falls, is reached from Highway 1. From Highway 61, turn North on Highway 1, heading inland toward Finland. Go 1.6 miles and park at the gravel pull-off on the left side of the road. A nearby sign says "Illgen Falls, Devil's Rock" and marks the head of the path.

HIKE DIFFICULTY
Easy
TRAIL QUALITY
Good
ROUND TRIP
0.3 mile
THE EXPERIENCE
★ ★ ★

A short gravel and boardwalk path takes you on a three-minute stroll to the top of the falls. You'll cross a gravel driveway that leads to a little log park building on your left. Continuing on and just past, you will come to the falls. From the top, Illgen Falls appears taller than it actually is, as the narrow but forceful cascade jettisons over a large rock ledge to a pool about 35 feet below. It is not a complicated falls, but impressive in its simplicity and power.

Illgen Falls

Table Rock Falls on a tributary to the Manitou

MANITOU RIVER
Crosby-Manitou State Park

Manitou River Falls

TRAILHEAD: To access the falls of Crosby-Manitou State Park, you must leave Highway 61 and head 6.5 miles up Highway 1 to where it intersects County Road 7 in Finland. Take a right on County Road 7 and continue 7.5 miles to the park entrance on the right side. Park maps are available at the informational display board, which also serves as the registration point for the hike-in campsites. Continue on to the parking area off the left side of the road, where three trailheads begin. On the left end of the parking area is the Humpback Trailhead. On the right is the Yellow Birch Trail. In the middle, Middle Trail begins. You will be taking this aptly named 'Middle Trail' which is part of the Superior Hiking Trail. A sign indicates distances to various intersecting trails, including "1.6 miles to the West Manitou River Trail," which is where we're going. This distance conflicts with other sources we consulted, however. We conclude that the distance to West Manitou River Trail is closest to 0.9 mile.

HIKE DIFFICULTY
Strenuous
TRAIL QUALITY
Poor
ROUND TRIP
2.3 miles
THE EXPERIENCE
★ ★ ★ ★

The Cascades

As you set off on Middle Trail, it is apparent that this trail is more rugged than those found in most state parks. It is well-worn, but there are many protruding rocks and roots. It begins ascending almost immediately. If you are taking this trail in late May to early June, you will see distinctive bellwort, yellow violets, and fragile-as-moonlight anemones. In mid-June, blue-bead lilies, starflowers, and false lily of the valley will mark your way. The understated and ephemeral spring flowers wear pale hues. It is easy to overlook these shy blooms amongst the dappled play of sun and

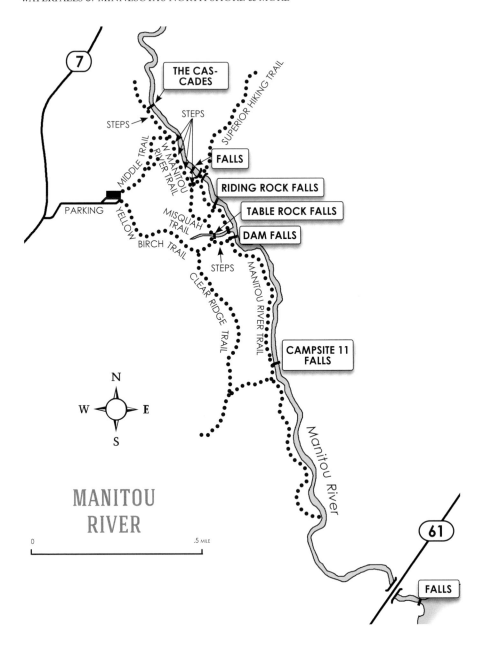

THE CAS-CADES

STEPS

STEPS

STEPS

SUPERIOR HIKING TRAIL

MIDDLE TRAIL

W. MANITOU RIVER TRAIL

FALLS

RIDING ROCK FALLS

TABLE ROCK FALLS

DAM FALLS

PARKING

YELLOW

MISQUAH TRAIL

BIRCH TRAIL

STEPS

CLEAR RIDGE TRAIL

MANITOU RIVER TRAIL

CAMPSITE 11 FALLS

N

W   E

S

MANITOU
RIVER

0   .5 MILE

Manitou River

61

FALLS

shadow upon the green. If you are both extremely fortunate and vigilant, you may encounter a moccasin flower (not as shy) as well. In early to mid-August, you will be treated to a bold display of beautiful pearl-like berries—red, white, blue, and orange, just poking up above the forest floor. Birch and evergreen rise above you. Pause a moment, take in the silence. This park is less traveled and well away from the steady drone of Highway 61. Even on a busy summer weekend, you will encounter few people, though you might find evidence of moose, bear or other north-woods denizens.

Middle Trail goes up and down and has some very steep inclines. There is the occasional boardwalk to keep your feet dry in muddy areas. About

The Cascades at high water

11 minutes into your hike, a sign indicates a spur path right to an overlook. To reach The Cascades, continue left on the Middle Trail Section of the Superior Hiking Trail, going up and down on natural steps of roots and on man-made steps of poles set into the inclines. You will come upon a shelter with a fire pit, one of the amenities of the Superior Hiking Trail. About 20 minutes into the hike, you will reach a sign where the Crosby Hill Trail branches off from the Middle Trail. Don't take it, but rather continue along Middle Trail and you will soon begin to hear The Cascades. As the trail continues on toward the Manitou River, you will descend along a very rocky stretch strewn with large boulders.

Twenty-five minutes into the hike, Middle Trail intersects with Manitou River Trail, which parallels the Manitou River. Go to the left. As you make your way over Medusa-like roots, you will hear the sirens of The Cascades calling you, their song getting louder with each step you take. You are still well above the river on this last leg, and you will catch glimpses of roiling white water beneath you. Forty challenging root and timber steps take you down to the river, where a promontory of rocks and boulders provides a view of the magnificent Manitou River Cascades.

The Cascades are composed of three phases, which together drop 40 to 50 feet along about a 150-foot stretch of river. The upper part of the falls is the narrowest and pours through a gorge and onto the middle tier, which is the largest and is comprised of multiple smaller falls. The lowest tier of the falls splits in two. If you visit

---

Manidowish *or* Manidobumadga-zibi *is Ojibwe for "spirit" or "ghost." It is believed that the heavy mist produced by some of the Manitou's falls may have contributed to this name.*

The Cascades during very high water, however, the tiers disappear and it all looks like one huge fall.

As always, be very cautious if you decide to move in for a more intimate experience with any waterfall. If you want to get closer to the heart of the Cascades, continue carefully on up the trail along the river. Be sure to give a wide berth to any precipitous drops. Maneuver the steps and roots and boulders to find yourself a perch at the brim of the falls. If it is July or August, and the river level is low, this may be along flat ledges, in the shadow of a tall rock wall at your back, and ancient cedar trees above. If it is during the lawless deluge of the Manitou's spring season, however, your seat will be several feet higher, because the ledges are submerged under several feet of gyrating water. Take a water and snack break while a cooling mist whirls round you with each shift of the breeze, and dragonflies coast through the air above the dancing white splashing.

Heading back along the River Trail, you will find yourself again at the Crosby Hill Trail intersection in about seven minutes. Ten more minutes can get you back to the overlook spur. Total return time from falls to parking lot is about 25 minutes. Be forewarned that the walk back can be grueling on a hot day. Much of it is uphill and you may not have the relief of a cooling Lake Superior breeze this far inland. It seemed to us that the hike back was twice as long as the hike to the falls, especially on a hot summer afternoon. It is obvious that much work has been done to improve this trail and the improvement is ongoing, but the nature of the terrain makes for a poor quality path and a difficult hike. In our opinion, though, the beauty of The Cascades makes the hike well worth the effort.

More Manitou River Falls

HIKE DIFFICULTY
Strenuous

TRAIL QUALITY
Poor

DISTANCE
from Campsite 3, along River Trail to Campsite 9 and back to parking 2.7 miles

THE EXPERIENCE
★★ to ★★★

If you are up for it, there are other notable falls on the Manitou River between The Cascades and Highway 61, though The Cascades is the best of the bunch. Most of these falls are located between campsites 4 and 9. (The southern quarter of Manitou River Trail, accessing campsites 13 to 16, contains no major falls.)

If you are continuing from The Cascades, turn around and go back downriver on the West Manitou River Trail. Pass the intersection with Middle Trail, staying on the West

Manitou River Trail. Our estimated walking times begin from this intersection. You will encounter river campsites, numbered 3 to 16 (1 and 2 are north of The Cascades).

As you make your way past this intersection, the trail rises high above the river with lots of rocks and log steps. Don't take the spur trail that goes to campsite 3. The trail will make its way back down to river level, and as you approach the spur trail to campsite 4, you will hear some rapids. There are no falls, though. Just past campsite 4, and about 10

The Cascades at low water

minutes past the Middle Trail intersection, you will cross a rustic wooden footbridge. This bridge passes over a creek which, in the spring, forms a slender falls that tumbles over the rocky creek bed.

After this crossing, the trail rises sharply again, climbing several dozen wooden steps to bring you high above the river. From here the trail goes up and down, making it a bit strenuous. About 20 minutes from Middle Trail, you will see a Superior Hiking Trail sign and a traditional, generic, brown and yellow trail sign 20 feet beyond that. Follow the Superior Hiking Trail, which turns sharply to the left and drops steeply down to the river. As you near the Manitou, there will be a short spur to the left where you will have a nice view upriver of two waterfalls that, along with a third just out of sight around the corner, we named "The Steps." The top two are the largest and drop about 10 to 15 feet over large, jagged boulders. When we were last there, the autumn scene was beautifully framed by the golden foliage of the aspen

The lovely spring woodland wildflower, bellwort, *is marked by yellow blooms appearing to be bowing in supplication. Leaves are often curled or twisted, giving the plant an almost wilted appearance.*

lining the river valley walls. The last waterfall of "The Steps" is at the Superior Hiking Trail Bridge, which is a one-minute walk down the main trail. The tea-colored falls drop about 6 feet along a boulder run of approximately 50 feet.

After enjoying the view from the bridge, continue down river on the west side. Take the informal trail that runs from the bridge along the river edge. A few minutes later, at campsite 5, is the waterfall we refer to as "Riding Rock Falls." The river pitches down about 6 feet, circling a 15-foot long wedge-shaped rock, topped with a tenacious cedar tree, before emptying into a quiet pool. Its shape invites you to sit astride the leading point of the outcrop, with water coursing on either side of the "ride." Tall hills float high in the distance. Continue past campsite 5, following the river's edge. Soon your path will be intersected by the Superior Hiking Trail coming in from the right. Keep going straight along the river, now on the Superior Hiking Trail. Seven minutes down river from campsite 5, small falls provide background music to a portion of the trail that is especially mossy and magical. Twisted roots worm their way at your feet and wildly contorted trunks of birch and cedar surround you. Side paths begin to appear when near the campsites. Some paths go to campsites and others skirt them. All follow the river at greater or lesser distances.

About 11 minutes after Riding Rock Falls, if you stay on river paths, look for a small waterfall coming in on the opposite bank where a side creek meets the Manitou. The path meets river's edge, and if you glance upstream at this juncture, you can see the falls.

About an hour beyond the intersection of Middle Trail and River Trail, you should reach campsite 7 (#6 is not on the river). This is where Yellow Birch Trail intersects the West Manitou River Trail. In just a few minutes, you will encounter the next notable falls on the Manitou. Follow the trail as it loops around a peninsula where the river takes a wide turn. You will come upon an unusual falls—simple but impressive. The top level of water is at eye-level, the drop being only about 4 feet. It flows in a thick, uninterrupted sheet over a wide, natural, dam-like shelf, visible through the water, as if through glass. Hence, we call it "Dam Falls." This effect is most stunning during high water periods.

You will cross a split log bridge over a small tributary stream, making its own mini waterfall as if warming up for the tumultuous concert ahead. This is a charming section of trail, mulched with pine needles and tiny pine cones. About nine minutes past Dam Falls, you will come upon campsite 8, where there are two small cascades about 75 feet apart. Each fall is a few feet high, the second being more impressive. Very large white pines tower above, carpeting the path with their needles. Right after this campsite, you will cross a small plank bridge. The trail turns right and then rises steeply up the bank. A small path to the right will take you into campsite 9. Go past this path and continue following the edge of the bluff downstream a very short way. Here, high above the Manitou, you will see another waterfall in the gorge below.

In our opinion, the waterfalls on the remaining length of the Manitou River are unimpressive. This is a good point at which to end your waterfall tour. (*For those who are more compulsive, see the directions in the paragraph below.) Return to the parking lot by going back to campsite 7 and taking the Yellow Birch Trail. You will be rewarded with the opportunity to see another small but enchanting waterfall on an unnamed creek. We would have missed it had we not paused for a breather and heard water falling like heavy rain. The trail rises steeply from campsite 7 to the crest of the river bluff. When you are about 100 feet from the top, just before the intersection of Yellow Birch and Misquah trails, you will see a spur trail heading off to the right. Follow it, and shortly a zigzagging wooden footbridge leads to a small creek that tumbles down the slope towards the Manitou. You will find a bench next to a 12-foot ribbon of water that falls into a pool and seems to almost disappear under the large rocks near the foot of the waterfall. One of these rocks is a large, flat square, so we named this Table Rock Falls. This grotto is filled with ferns, mosses, and boulders. The twisted roots and trunks of old cedars seem to spring out of the rock.

*Only one other notable waterfall is left in this stretch. About one-half mile farther and four minutes past campsite 11, this waterfall spans the river and descends in several steps, each several feet high, over an 80-foot run of water. Right after these last falls, there is a trail intersection. A sign indicates the dead end of River Trail ahead and campsites 13 to 16. Go right instead, where you will soon reach another intersection and a sign for Matt Willis Trail and Cedar Ridge Trail. Go right on Cedar Ridge Trail. Notice how the vegetation changes around you as you pass beneath lovely maple trees. Thirteen minutes past the intersection, there is a wooden bench with a footrest and an awesome view out over the trees and hills to Lake Superior on the horizon. Rest awhile; you've earned it. Twenty more minutes of hiking will bring you to the intersection of Yellow Birch Trail—the trail that leads to home. Head left on Yellow Birch; a creek will parallel your way for a time. Nine minutes past the last intersection, you will encounter Benson Lake Trail, going off to your left. Don't take it. Head on, and you can reach your car about an hour after heading back from campsite 12, or three hours after setting off from the intersection of Middle Trail and River Trail.

The moccasin flower *is a rare beauty of the northern coniferous forests. A member of the lady-slipper family, its unique maroon flower offers insects entry through a cleft in its base, and exit only after moving up through the flower's stamens and pistil. Thus, pollination is achieved as the insect makes its escape.*

Falls at Manitou's Mouth

TRAILHEAD: Charter a boat at Tofte or Beaver Bay.

HIKE DIFFICULTY Easy to Queasy
TRAIL QUALITY Calm to high seas
DISTANCE ROUND TRIP 8 miles
THE EXPERIENCE ★★★★★

This waterfall is on private property. The only public access is via Lake Superior, which offers a unique and dramatic perspective of the only major waterfall along Minnesota's North Shore that drops directly into the lake. We found ourselves, the last weekend of September, looking for a boat. Our sea-savvy publisher had already put his boat up for the winter and warned us that if we ventured out on the lake this late in the season, to "Be careful."

After some phone calls, we found a willing and able captain, Darren Peck of Tofte Charters, to schedule a time the following week for our waterfall quest—the last remaining waterfall on the North Shore we had yet to visit. "Actually," he said, "the weather is beautiful today. I'm free, and the further into fall we get, the iffier the weather becomes." After a short discussion, my husband and I agreed to meet him at Taconite Harbor in four hours (that's how long it takes us to dash up from St. Cloud to the Shore).

Three hours later, we passed Duluth. Numerous sailboats glided across the peaceful lake and we congratulated ourselves on "striking while the iron is hot" or, more appropriately, "making hay while the sun shines," and being spontaneous enough to drop everything and head up north while the weather was with us. Finally, the tune which had been going through my mind all the way from St. Cloud, "The Wreck of the Edmund Fitzgerald," especially the line, "Superior, they said, never gives up her dead when the gales of November come early," faded from my mind. But an hour later, as we pulled in at the Taconite Harbor boat launch, the previously calm lake now sported whitecaps.

Our captain was there with his boat, but he said, "Just half an hour after you called, the wind picked up. I don't think it looks too good. But we can go out a ways and then decide whether we should go for it or turn back."

Then he asked, "Do you get seasick?"

As the boat bucked its way across 3- to 5-foot waves, I felt compelled to say, "Don't feel like we have to do this just because we drove four hours. If it's not safe,

The mouth of the Manitou

you can turn around. You're the captain. Of course, it goes without saying that you're the one that knows best if it's safe." Or some such blather.

"I wouldn't go if it weren't safe," he replied tolerantly.

Okay, I knew that. I settled in to enjoy the view and noted that this was just like the jet boat rides we had taken at Wisconsin Dells or Niagara Falls, but without the speed. Plenty of bumps and thrills, though. The view of the North Shore from the lake was gorgeous, especially with fall colors burnishing the trees. The yellows and oranges seemed to melt down onto the rock faces along the shore, clad in their own autumn-hued lichens.

We hit some notably bigger swells. Darren explained that we were experiencing "sisters." These are larger waves that occur in groups of two to three. In this case, they were 6-footers. "One theory," he said, "is that the Edmund Fitzgerald went down because of 'sisters.' The boat was 729 feet long and it hit two 30-footers and broke in half." I silently estimated the length of our boat and found that dang song coming back into my mind.

When you see the North Shore from the lake, mostly it looks as if Highway 61 doesn't exist—the forested hills appear to stretch up and away to those mysterious places where wolves roam and moose ramble. Superior meets the land on beaches or rocky outcrops or cliff faces that look as though someone took giant bites out of the shoreline. Looking up or down lake, hills rise one behind the other, the nearest darker than the farthest, the lake's breath enveloping the most distant peaks in mist. The nub of Palisade Head is ghostly in the distance. This vista rivals the scenic coastlines of California, another great place where the primal elements of earth and water meet.

"If these waves were coming from the other direction, we wouldn't be going. It'll be easier on the way back." Darren's voice broke my reveries. "This wind is coming from the southwest. The biggest waves are the northeasters that gather their strength along the whole lake."

I was impressed with Darren's deft handling of the boat. His subtle maneuverings allowed us to make headway against the waves, quartering into them, not pounding them head-on. I could see that the timing of his movements, his reading of the waves, and his anticipation of what lay ahead is an art.

The sky was blue with only a few cobwebby clouds. A half-hour into our voyage, we passed Sugarloaf Cove. A little less than an hour out and we passed the point where the Caribou River enters the lake, the dip of its valley visible at treeline. As we approached the Manitou, the waves became slightly larger, but we were now only a mile away from our destination and we were going for it.

The Manitou River waterfall at Lake Superior lived up to all of our expectations. A mighty volume of water emerges from a shadowy chasm above, framed by cedars hanging off the cliffs, and crashes about 20 feet, vertically, into the lake. A large rock protrudes in the midst of the maelstrom, deflecting some of the rush and adding to the clouds of smoky mist rolling off of the torrent. The scene is set in a small cove, with a sandbar that may move daily, Darren told us, depending upon the whim of the water, the wind, and the lake. On this day the bar was just in front of the waterfall. Some days it shifts diagonally, channeling the Manitou's currents through a mysterious rock arch flanking the right side of the cove.

Our captain explained that the very humid microclimate created in the enclosed cove was especially conducive to ferns and mosses, unusual vegetation to be growing so close to the lake. As if on cue, and to punctuate the exceptional nature of this place, two bald eagles soared into view above the scene. Darren pointed out a blow-hole along the rocky waterline to the right of the cove, where water was apparently pushed deep into cavernous rock and then forcefully expelled. The similarities to the Pacific coast now extended even to these blasts of water, though here they weren't caused by whales.

This waterfall warranted our anticipation. It was a fitting finale to our project—a waterfall pouring into Lake Superior—where all these rollicking rivers end. The boat ride back was comparatively smooth because we were running with the waves. It's amazing that when you go in the direction that Lake Superior wants you to go, she shows a totally different face than when you oppose her. You can surf along with her wavy rhythm—the water appearing almost calm—or you can go against the waves and fight her. Husbands take note.

Our boat skimmed toward home across water 100 feet deep. The depth goes to 800 feet, two miles out. Darren has seen surface water temperatures drop from 70 degrees to 36 in one day—when the wind blows away the water warmed by long summer days of sun, as if they had never taken place. Respect Superior. And if you embark on a voyage to this Manitou waterfall, find a capable captain!

Fireweed *grows in open areas, especially where there has been a forest fire or recent disturbance. The pink/lavender blooms taper to a point on a 2- to 4-foot stalk. Seeds are carried on the breeze, like dandelions, making it an especially prolific wildflower.*

Caribou Falls

CARIBOU RIVER
Caribou Falls State Wayside Park

Caribou Falls

TRAILHEAD: The Highway 61 parking area for the Caribou Falls trailhead is located on the east bank of the Caribou River 5 miles northeast of Little Marais near mile marker 70. Embark at the Superior Hiking Trail sign.

HIKE DIFFICULTY
Moderate
TRAIL QUALITY
Fair to Poor
ROUND TRIP
1 mile
THE EXPERIENCE
★ ★ ★ ★

The well-worn dirt path to Caribou Falls rambles through birch and evergreen along the murmuring Caribou River. This shallow river has a different feel than most of the North Shore rivers. Crystal clear water runs over and around a bed of rich red rocks, creating wonderful places to sit and contemplate the pools, eddies, and mini falls.

A few minutes beyond the parking lot, a spur leading to the Superior Hiking Trail heads off to the right. An old, badly eroded trail, now closed, went along the river's edge. Follow the Superior Hiking Trail, which rises well above the river. There are no railings, so take care not to get too close to the edge. One-half mile into the hike, you will come to a trail going left and 156 steps down to the base of Caribou Falls.

At the base of awesome Caribou Falls, a sand and pebble spit juts out, letting you walk to within 20 feet of the cascade, depending on the water level. The river pounds white through a narrow notch 40 feet above, turns right, then plunges down into a saucer-like pool. One section at the top of the falls shoots forcefully outward as if blasted by a firefighter's high-powered hose. The scene is set in a rounded basin surrounded by high black rock walls and verdant trees. After a leisurely sojourn here, you can walk back to the parking lot in 15 minutes.

Before the woodland caribou *were extirpated from the state, it is probable that they may have been found in this river valley; hence the name of the river.*

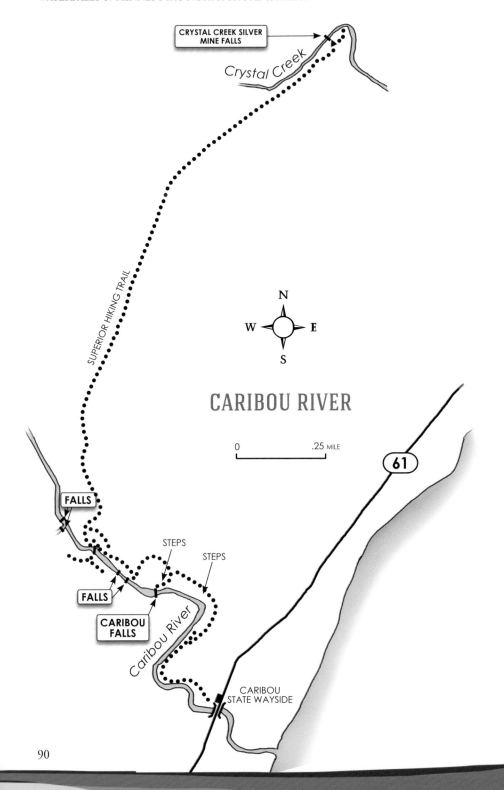

CRYSTAL CREEK SILVER MINE FALLS

Crystal Creek

SUPERIOR HIKING TRAIL

N
W   E
S

CARIBOU RIVER

0   .25 MILE

61

FALLS

STEPS

STEPS

FALLS

CARIBOU FALLS

Caribou River

CARIBOU STATE WAYSIDE

More Caribou River Falls

While Caribou Falls is the river's most spectacular water-fall, there are more falls a short way up the path. From the base of Caribou Falls, retrace your steps back up the wooden stairs. Continue upstream on the Superior Hiking Trail. Near the top of your climb an observation deck is perched on the edge of the canyon wall. Far below you can see the top of Caribou Falls. You also get a wonderful panoramic view of Lake Superior floating on the horizon. Continuing upstream, the smell of pine, the sounds of birdsong, and the rushing river accompany your climb on the pinecone-strewn trail. The canyon is too high and steep to see much of the river flowing below, but five minutes above the intersection of the steps down to Caribou Falls, you can hear and see a second waterfall. Just above that one is a third waterfall, which plunges into a large basin worn round by the swirling river. Unfortunately, there is no river access to either of these falls, but the precarious view from above is impressive anyway. Be careful!

HIKE DIFFICULTY
Easy
TRAIL QUALITY
Fair
ROUND TRIP
0.4 mile from
Caribou Falls to
bridge
THE EXPERIENCE
★ ★

Less than a minute later, and 0.2 mile above Caribou Falls, you will encounter a bridge spanning the river. A falls just below this bridge plunges over red rock and into a narrow ravine. Looking upriver from the bridge, another falls tumbles from two directions around a rocky island, dropping about 15 feet.

You are likely to encounter bunchberry *on your North Shore hikes. You will come to recognize its distinctive whorl of deeply veined, elliptical leaves topped by what appears to be a white four-petaled flower. The actual flower, however, is in the center of these, while the part that appears to be the petals are other flower parts called "bracts." The flowers will evolve into a "bunch" of brilliant red berries as the summer progresses.*

Crystal Creek pours through an old mine.

CRYSTAL CREEK
Near Caribou Falls State Wayside Park

Crystal Creek Falls

TRAILHEAD: Crystal Creek is best accessed from the Caribou Falls State Wayside Park on Highway 61, 5 miles east of Little Marais, near mile marker 70. Embark at the Superior Hiking Trail sign by the parking lot. **Note:** *See Caribou River map, page 90.*

HIKE DIFFICULTY
Strenuous
TRAIL QUALITY
Fair to Poor
ROUND TRIP
4 miles from Caribou Falls trailhead; 2.6 miles from bridge above Caribou Falls
THE EXPERIENCE
★ ★

We hesitate to recommend this waterfall hike, but the waterfall is mentioned by other sources and is very unusual. The reason we're not enthused about this hike is because the final leg to the falls is extremely difficult and potentially dangerous. Please read the entire hike description before making a decision. If, after that, you are still determined to see this waterfall (rather than just looking at our photo, which is much easier and safer), follow the previous directions to the bridge 0.2 mile beyond Caribou Falls.

After the bridge, the trail soon veers right along a side creek. This is a pleasant stretch on a fairly level dirt path. An open birch canopy allows for sun-loving wildflowers, such as devil's paintbrush and flowering raspberry in July. Eighteen minutes after leaving the bridge the trail crosses a power line clearing, where you can see distant Lake Superior, then heads back into the woods, which now includes large conifers and towering paper birch. Seven minutes later the trail descends to a plank bridge crossing a creek, and then continues through a thick birch forest carpeted with ferns. Looking around, all you can see is the white and black of birch bark with few, if any, gaps in the backdrop. Three minutes later you will see a covered bridge spanning Crystal Creek. If it is July or August chances are good that the creek bed will appear bone dry. Closer inspection will reveal tiny trickles and small pools where water striders skate in search of the abundant mosquitoes. Unless there is a good flow of water in the creek, continuing the hike down to the waterfall is not worth the reward.

The trail to the waterfall is on your right, just before the covered bridge on the west side of the creek. It is actually a signed spur trail leading to a Superior Hiking Trail campsite about 100 yards downstream. From this campsite, perched above the creek, a short path to the left takes you down the bank to the streambed. A sign here reads, "Old Mine in Creek." This sign raises intense curiosity to see the mine. You can peer into the creek gorge (which is lovely from above) and see that something went on down there long ago and that something cool is going on with the water now. But trying to climb down to the waterfall is not so cool. We offer the following information so you can make an informed decision about exploring the gorge.

From here, the stream drops steeply and disappears into a large opening in the rock. This hole is the collapsed ceiling of an old silver mine. The rock here is very unusual for the North Shore, with large veins of white quartz. We tried climbing down the streambed to get a better look at the waterfall, but it was too steep and slippery, even though the water level was low. We later discovered a somewhat less dangerous (but equally strenuous) route down to the waterfall and mine.

From the campsite (not the stream bed), continue on the other small trail that heads downstream and then peters out in about 30 yards. There is no path down to the waterfall and you cannot see it from above. You may be tempted to try getting down to the creek, but resist the temptation—it's too steep. Instead, head away from the stream a short distance and then go downhill where the incline is less severe. Bushwhack and traverse your way down the steep, 60-degree hillside, clinging for your dear life to any trees or roots you can find. Be extra careful, because some trees that appear solid are actually rotten. If you begin sliding, you may not be able to stop until you reach the bottom—and you may get hurt.

Once you reach the creek bed, walk upstream a short distance to where the creek exits from a small cave-like opening. Peer into the darkness where you'll see delicate strands of water, illuminated from above, spilling 6 feet from the aperture in the mine roof. It is unfortunate that this unique waterfall is so hard to approach.

Two Island River Falls near the railroad trestle

TWO ISLAND RIVER

Taconite Harbor

Lower Two Island Falls

TRAILHEAD: Heading northeast on Highway 61, near a small sign that says #8324, pull off to the right, 100 feet before the Two Island River sign and just before the railroad trestle, by the broken gate. An old stop sign marks what used to be a road.

HIKE DIFFICULTY
Easy
TRAIL QUALITY
Fair
ROUND TRIP
0.2 mile
THE EXPERIENCE
★★ to ★★★

Cross the highway and follow it over the river. The narrow, hard-to-descend trail begins 20 feet beyond the river. Step over the highway barrier. The grassy path through shrubbery exists only because human feet have trampled one. If water is low, you can make your way upriver on the rock outcropping at the edge of the riverbed. But if the Two Island is filled to the brink, follow fisherman trails a few yards away from the bank. Head upriver about 400 feet to an old railroad trestle. Beware of rusty barbed wire on the ground just before crossing.

Across the trestle, a low concrete wall provides convenient seating from which to view the two-tiered Lower Two Island Falls. This waterfall would warrant another star, if only it could levitate and fly to a site with fewer signs of human disturbance. The upper portion spills 12 feet through beige and black rock, and the lower drops about 10 feet into a square pool. The river then flows through two culverts beneath the railroad tracks. If you've a yen to clamber down to water level, you can do so fairly easily via rocks to the right of the lower pool.

On your way back to the highway bridge, note some small waterfalls and an interesting series of potholes just upriver from the highway and on the southwest side

*One of the few orange wildflowers you will see on the North Shore is the non-native "*devil's paint brush*" (or less interesting-sounding, "Orange Hawkweed,"—it is considered a weed by some). It flaunts beautiful, sunset- orange flowers atop a small unassuming plant, somewhat resembling a small dandelion.*

The Upper Falls

of the river, below the trestle. Don't be too startled by the giant human toe prints in the lowest pool on the left side of the river.

Upper Two Island Falls

HIKE DIFFICULTY
Easy (if you drive,
except for the
bumps)

TRAIL QUALITY
Poor, as a road
Fair, as a hike

ROUND TRIP
1.0 mile from
Hwy. 61

THE EXPERIENCE
★ ★ ★

TRAILHEAD: About 200 feet southwest of where the Two Island River crosses under Highway 61, you can drive uphill along the rough 0.5-mile gravel and grass "road" through aspen and pine. Park in a gravel turnaround where the road ends just before the railroad tracks. From there, you can easily make your way to the base of the upper portion of Two Island Falls. Walk from your car up onto the tracks and head to the right about 100 feet, where the river crosses under the rail bed. The falls will be visible just upstream from here.

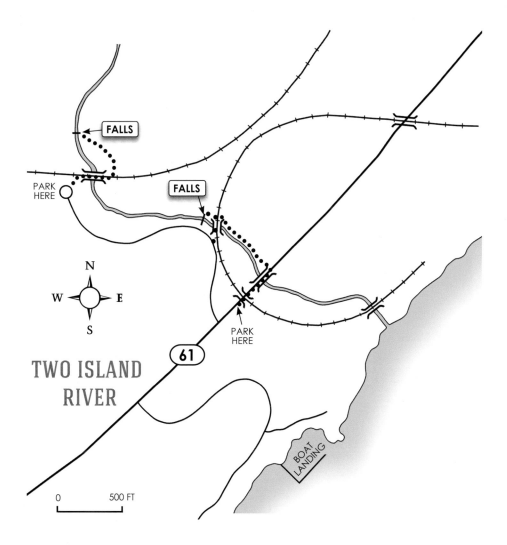

FALLS

FALLS

PARK
HERE

PARK
HERE

N
W · E
S

61

TWO ISLAND
RIVER

BOAT
LANDING

0   500 FT

The upper level of Two Island Falls promises to be a rather spectacular sight in times of high water. Low water reveals the 25-foot waterfall to be a long purpley-hued slide—an interesting mixture of red and black—over jutting rock shelves and two potholes. It also features a convenient outcrop area from which to view the watery confluence.

Cross River Falls

CROSS RIVER

Cross River Wayside, Schroeder

Cross River Falls

TRAILHEAD: You can see Cross River Falls from the Highway 61 bridge. Pull into the parking area across from Schroeder's Cross River Heritage Center, on the west side of the river. This impressive falls flows down the red rock face at eye level from the bridge. To the right of the main flow is a small pool in a lovely pothole grotto where ferns and other foliage grow. You can look into the river ravine from the lake side of the bridge.

HIKE DIFFICULTY
Easy
TRAIL QUALITY
Good
ROUND TRIP
< 0.1 mile
THE EXPERIENCE
★ ★ ★ ★

More Cross River Falls

TRAILHEAD: The other falls on the Cross River are not as easily accessible as the one off Highway 61. About 100 yards east of the river, just opposite what is now an antique shop, Skou Road heads inland from the highway. Travel 0.2 mile up this road to a small parking area on the right. You will see a sign for the Superior Hiking Trail on the north end of the parking lot.

HIKE DIFFICULTY
Strenuous
TRAIL QUALITY
Fair
ROUND TRIP
3 miles
THE EXPERIENCE
★ ★

From the Superior Hiking Trail trailhead, take the left fork to Superior Ridge. In about five minutes, you will pass a map and a sign that lets you know you're on "Spur Trail." Ten minutes from the parking lot, you will pass a shelter and reach another fork in the path. Don't take the left fork, which leads to a bridge. Instead, stay right, on the Spur Trail. About 10 or 15 minutes later, at the top of a small rise, the trail goes to the

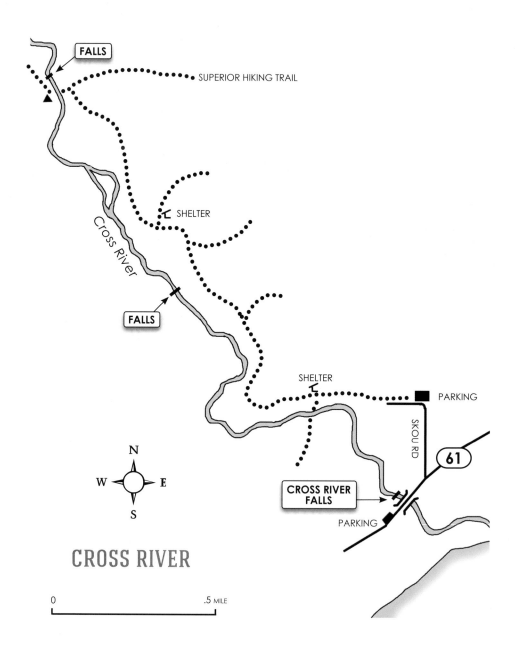

FALLS

SUPERIOR HIKING TRAIL

SHELTER

Cross River

FALLS

SHELTER

PARKING

SKOU RD

61

N
W E
S

CROSS RIVER
FALLS

PARKING

CROSS RIVER

0   .5 MILE

left and you will see an old portion of the Superior Hiking Trail heading off directly to your right. (If you come to the second shelter, you've gone too far.)

By now you can hear lots of things going on down in the river that sound like huge waterfalls or rapids. So near and yet so far away! That sound will continue to tantalize you. You will swear you are passing magnificent falls far below, but can't get to them. Or can you?

This stretch of the Cross starts out as a river with gently sloping banks. As you head upriver, the banks rise and become steep canyon walls. Once the trail brings you above the canyon, access to the river becomes impossible. In other words, exploration off the trail may result in you tumbling off a cliff and over the brink. We are continually amazed, however, that when we dare an adventurous, but very, very cautious expedition down to a waterfall, we often find an angler already there, with all his gear, apparently via a path known only to anglers. On more than one occasion, one of these wise souls has watched us try to find our way back up, taken mercy on us, and kindly directed us to a path that then becomes all too apparent. We embrace these directions with undying gratitude, and when we reach the top, look at each other and grumble, "Duh!"

That's just what happened to us at the Cross River. After meeting a local at a nearby art gallery and expressing our frustration at hearing so many falls rumbling down in the canyon, but being unable to access them, he smiled slyly and said, "Oh, you can get down there." He didn't tell us how to get there, but we were determined to find the way.

This was our meandering route: At the second shelter, we backtracked diagonally, along the slope of the hill (giving wide berth to any steep drop-offs) in the direction of the river. We traversed and fern-whacked. In seven minutes, we were almost to the river when we saw the tell-tale dirt path, "Duh!" and two fly-fishermen. We think the more direct route down to the waterfall begins about one minute before the second shelter, opposite an old portion of the Superior Hiking Trail (probably predating it as a fisherman's trail), which heads up and away from the river. Nevertheless, even this route necessitates some fern-whacking.

Making our way upstream along a gray and pink rock outcropping, we were rewarded with the sight of a lovely little waterfall located where the canyon walls begin to rise and cedars hang precipitously above like living wall sconces. Going upstream beyond this falls requires wading. The waterfall is about 8 to 10 feet high, drops vertically, and seemingly appears out of nowhere: yet another North Shore

Waterfall deep in the Cross River canyon

gem. With the help of the kind fishermen, we made our way back to the upper main trail (we soon lost the fisherman's trail) in six minutes.

Once back on the main trail and just past the second shelter, you can hear the aforementioned waterfall. Two minutes later, you can barely see some more falls through the trees. This large, three-tiered waterfall (by our estimates) drops 30-40 feet. Someone ought to build an observation platform here. With a clear shot, we excitedly concluded this waterfall would earn at least four stars and may surpass the Cross River waterfall on Highway 61 as the best falls on the river. From this falls on, any tantalizing sounds you hear from the river are best ignored. The treacherous cliffs are not necessarily apparent through the trees and heavy undergrowth on the upper bluff. You can't make your way down to the river.

Forty-three minutes into your walk you will come to a river overlook and a sign that reads, "1.5 miles from parking area on Spur Trail." There's even a bench to sit upon. Look to the right and you'll see the last waterfall upriver. This view is very satisfactory. For a closer look, start walking. Ten minutes will get you there. Head left along the river, take a short flight of steps, and within a couple of minutes you will come to another fork, at which you go right. The way is now rocky, but carefully placed steps will help you along, as well as a short flight of stairs that is more like a hybrid ladder. This leads to a wooden footbridge, fording a small, but interesting falls where the water flows from the left side of the river into a kind of trench along the right-hand side.

Cross the bridge and head right, toward the waterfalls you saw from above. You will see signs for camping and several campsites, and will find yourself at the falls approximately one hour after starting out from the trailhead. The water pours down a 45-degree shelf about 20 feet into a quiet pool beneath. Seek and you may find the natural spiral staircase of roots and rock that takes you down to a lovely spot to sit and regard the orb-like basin around you, carved from highly fractured rock with moss highlighting the cracks. Sit at water's edge and watch the sudsy foam designs float past with their corresponding shadows on the shallow-edged, but deepening bowl of the river bottom. Small caves, ground by the river, are also visible from this perch.

If you venture farther up the now level trail from this last waterfall, it crosses a small creek and follows the river on a winding, shaded path, even edged in stretches by hand-placed stones. You will find that the falls you saw is really the lower section of a series of cascades that come from up and around a corner. When you have taken it all in, you can make the return trip to your vehicle in about 45 minutes.

Local history tells the story of a missionary priest and his Native American guides who were caught in a violent storm while crossing Lake Superior in a canoe to visit Ojibwe along the North Shore. They were able to make a safe landing at the mouth of what was ever after called "Cross River" or Tchibaitago-zibi—"Wood of the Soul," after the wooden cross they fashioned there, in an expression of gratitude to the Divine. Today, a granite cross marks the spot.

One of several scenic falls on the Temperance

TEMPERANCE RIVER
Temperance River State Park

Temperance River Falls

TRAILHEAD: Parking for the Temperance River is on both sides of Highway 61, near mile marker 80. The sign marking the beginning of "Cauldron Trail" is on the east side of the river, on the east end of the upper parking lot.

Hidden Falls and others

From the parking lot, Cauldron Trail heads up the river. Though the river first resembles a long pool, it is soon apparent that the Temperance is anything but calm. The trail curves to the left and you can see the river emerge from the base of a tall and narrow chasm. Look more closely and you'll see a waterfall churning in the dark recesses of the gorge. This is the aptly named "Hidden Falls."

This trail features marvelous vista viewpoints masterfully crafted from stone by the Civilian Conservation Corps in the 1930s overlooking the tense scenery of the Temperance. Follow the trail around the river bend. When you reach the base of a small cliff, the trail goes left or right. To the left is the first of seven overlooks, where you have a closer look at the shadowy Hidden Falls. Enjoy the view, then head back to the trail and go right. You will climb approximately 40 rock steps through a somber, winding gap in the rock, reminiscent of steps emerging from a dungeon.

HIKE DIFFICULTY
Moderately strenuous
TRAIL QUALITY
Good
ROUND TRIP
1.4 miles to
Upper Falls
THE EXPERIENCE
★ ★ ★ ★

The well-suited Ojibwe name for the Temperance River *was Kawinbash, meaning "deep hollow." The present-day, anglicized name refers to the absence of a "bar" at its mouth.*

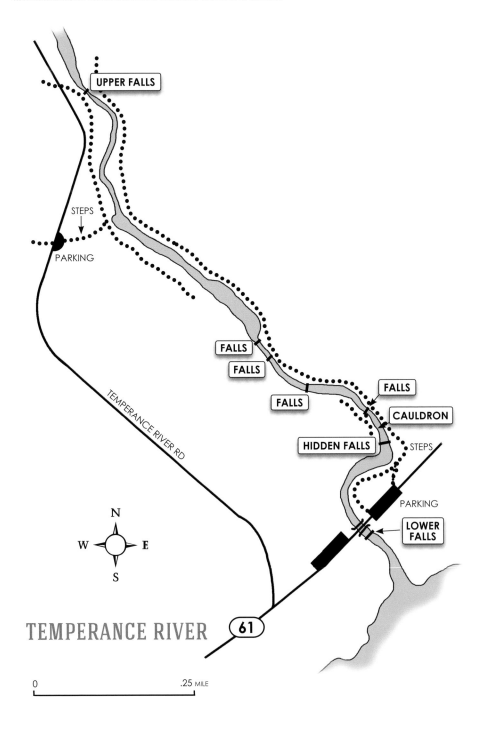

UPPER FALLS

STEPS

PARKING

FALLS

FALLS

FALLS

FALLS

CAULDRON

HIDDEN FALLS

STEPS

PARKING

LOWER FALLS

TEMPERANCE RIVER RD

N
W ◈ E
S

TEMPERANCE RIVER   61

0   .25 MILE

Hidden Falls

The dramatic canyon walls rise so steeply that in many places you cannot see the river from above. Proceed, crossing a barren rock outcropping ornamented with dwarf evergreens. You will come to a dramatic overlook, and a ledge below it with another overlook. The latter lets you peer into a roiling "cauldron"—a pothole formed over time by swirling sand, gravel, and water pounding in from above. There has been a succession of such potholes over the geological history of the river. The gradual connection of these holes has resulted in a canyon with scalloped walls. Looking upstream, a footbridge spans the gorge where the river pours through yet another chute.

You can cross the footbridge to the west bank, but we find that the east bank trail offers the best views of the falls. One minute and 12 stone steps below the footbridge, there are two overlooks of yet another falls, about 15 feet in height. Walk up the path a few minutes more and you'll come to a balcony-like overlook along the river's edge. This overlook is adjacent to a series of falls and slides dropping 12 feet over a ledge. At the bottom is a cave shaped by time and the Temperance's powerful currents. Looking upriver, you can see more falls, above which the river and terrain appear to level out. These falls feature a multi-tiered cascade and lots of places to lounge around on rocks.

If you have the energy, continue walking upriver. (If you don't, driving instructions to the upper falls of the Temperance follow.) You won't encounter as many people above this point, making for a quieter hike. The trail continues to be smooth with occasional rocks. Soon you will walk up a steep, but short hill where the trail wanders away from the river's edge. About a quarter of a mile upstream, the trail gradually finds its way back to the Temperance. You'll start to hear rushing water as the river nears. An informal path heads left through the bushes, dropping sharply down to the river. The upper falls begin by forcing their way through narrow channels and over shelves, converging quickly in a wider channel that drops about 10 feet over a 30-foot run. At low water levels, the upper falls has tame areas for refreshing, late summer dips, but the river's ferocity is unleashed when water is high. Though you may occasionally see those folks who are unable to resist a swim in the Temperance, be aware that people have paid with their lives for doing so. Always exercise extreme caution, even when sticking just a toe into these wild waters.

The Upper Falls by car

The Upper Falls of the Temperance River are also accessible by car and a short hike. Turn north off Highway 61 0.2 mile west of the Temperance River on the Temperance River Road. Follow this road 0.7 mile and pull into a small, unmarked parking area. Proceed on the dirt path heading toward the river. At the bottom of a small run of steps, go left to the falls. When you are coming back, be sure to turn right, up the stairs, at the fork in the trail. It takes about eight minutes to return from the upper end of this small series of falls to the parking area.

Lower Falls

TRAILHEAD: Park in the parking area for the Temperance River on Highway 61. You can park on either side of the road, but if you are just going to look at this waterfall, it would be best to park on the lake side.

HIKE DIFFICULTY
Poor to Moderate
TRAIL QUALITY
Easy
ROUND TRIP
< 0.1 mile
THE EXPERIENCE
★ ★

This is a modest waterfall of which few are aware, both due to its location and the presence of so many mightier waterfalls on the Temperance River. Nevertheless, in the interest of being thorough, we mention it here.

Head west from the parking lot, cross the bridge, and take the 25 railroad tie and slate steps to river's edge. You'll see the underbelly of the highway bridge, and it's not pretty. But if you use your imagination, you may see the ruins of a castle rather than the vestiges of a walkway that has fallen into disrepair in the face of a ruthless river. We visited at a time of low water, and it is likely that when the water is higher, this route is impassable. As it is, watch your step!

The bridge itself has been reinforced with girders on the upriver side, presumably to prevent the whole bridge from succumbing to the temper of the Temperance. It's shadowy and dank beneath the bridge, but we saw no trolls dwelling there. What we did see was a waterfall plunging about 15 feet, deflected into a pothole on its wild way down.

Largest Falls on the Onion River

ONION RIVER
Ray Berglund Memorial Wayside

Onion River Falls

TRAILHEAD: Park at the wayside, located 4 miles northeast of Tofte on the northeast side of the Onion River, near mile marker 86 and the Cliff Dweller Inn.

HIKE DIFFICULTY
Moderate
TRAIL QUALITY
Fair
ROUND TRIP
0.8 mile
THE EXPERIENCE
★★ to ★★★★

Climb the steps to the newly improved trail, past a cleared brushy area beneath power lines. Head right along the trail above the river, as it continues through birch and conifer trees. There have been many improvements to the Onion River Falls trails since the first edition of this book. Paths are wide with a packed dirt surface, much of which is also overlaid with finely ground material that hardens to a cement-like surface. In addition, whole sections of the path and overlooks are beautifully edged with set stonework. Many hours of work have been dedicated to make this trail almost as impressive as the Onion Falls themselves.

About five minutes into the hike, a 15-foot spur trail heads left to an overlook of the river and some of its falls below. Be very careful. There are no guardrails and it is a big drop to the river. From here, the trail makes a gradual climb and the sound of the river intensifies. A minute later, you'll find another short spur to a precipitous overlook of the rowdy Onion. As the trail continues its gentle ascent, you will encounter various river and waterfall vistas from lofty promontories. Within a few minutes, the path swings to the right, away from the river, to skirt a large ravine. When it returns to the rim of the river bluff, you will be overlooking the top of the large waterfall that you saw previously from a distance. From the overlook, another path goes back downriver and descends the riverbank, eventually taking you down to the water's edge just below the waterfall. This path is steep and loose in places, and if you choose to risk it, be very careful. The waterfall drops 15 feet in two steps into a paisley-shaped pool. Most of the flow cuts beneath the cliff wall on the far side of the falls. Sheer, gray walls surround the paisley pool, highlighted in places with

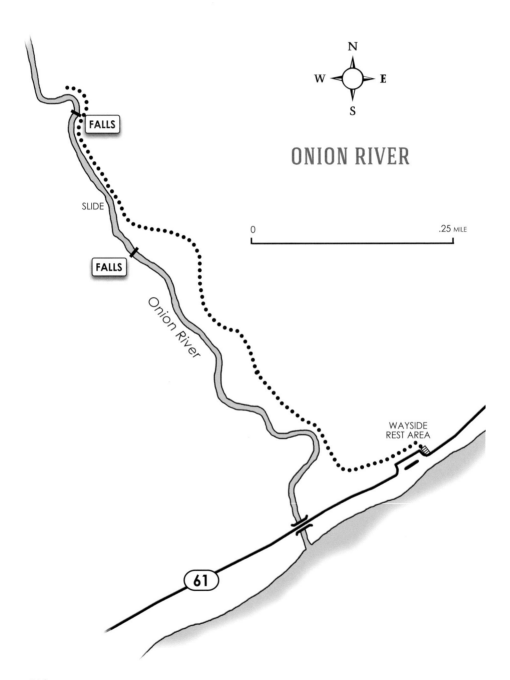

ONION RIVER

FALLS

SLIDE

FALLS

Onion River

N
W ◆ E
S

0 .25 MILE

WAYSIDE
REST AREA

61

white calcite veins. After lingering in the pool a moment, the water drops another 9 feet and tumbles downstream.

Back on the main trail, as you climb farther upriver, you will have outstanding views of the river's long, impressive slide approaching the waterfall. The trek to the next overlook takes several minutes. The river makes a calm "S" turn before its riotous descent. The well-trod trail continues. Look over your shoulder for majestic views of the Onion River valley with Lake Superior on the horizon. It took us about 20 minutes to reach trail's end at an abandoned bridge. Turn around and retrace your steps, now gently descending. You may be tempted, as others have, to obtain a water's edge view of the Onion's falls. Various scary side paths skid down sheer slopes to the river. We won't recommend any of them. Including time spent watching an unidentifiable (to us) brown animal make its way through the rocky chasm below, our round trip excursion lasted less than an hour.

The Onion River *was named after the abundance of wild onions growing in the woods along the river years ago.*

Upper Falls on the Poplar River

POPLAR RIVER

Lutsen

Upper Falls

TRAILHEAD: Head off of Highway 61, up County Road 5, or "Ski Hill Road," about 1.8 miles, to the Lutsen ski hill. Go to the end of the road, past the gondola parking. There is parking to your left, designated with a Superior Hiking Trail sign.

HIKE DIFFICULTY
Easy
TRAIL QUALITY
Good
ROUND TRIP
0.8 mile
THE EXPERIENCE
★ ★ ★

Head left on the trail, at this point a wide dirt road. Four minutes into the walk, the trail splits. Take the left fork to South Oberg parking, not to Caribou. Three minutes later, you will reach the bridge crossing the Poplar River and the falls. From the bridge, you behold a really lovely vista of the Poplar River. In the distance, up on the hillside, you can see the ski facilities tucked amongst the trees. Just above the bridge, the Poplar River narrows, surging through a 3-foot chute between huge rocks. Descending beneath the bridge, the river slightly widens, though still only to 10 to 15 feet, as it follows a terraced course downhill, framed by evergreen and birch, spilling steeply over and around mammoth boulders. Six minutes will have you back at your car.

Middle Falls

TRAILHEAD: Where Highway 61 crosses over the Poplar River, there is a footbridge on the north side of the highway. Pull off to park on either side of this footbridge. Walk onto the footbridge and peer down into the Poplar River to see a waterfall in the form of a long slide almost directly below you. It continues

HIKE DIFFICULTY
Easy
TRAIL QUALITY
Good
ROUND TRIP
< 0.1 mile
THE EXPERIENCE
★ to ★ ★

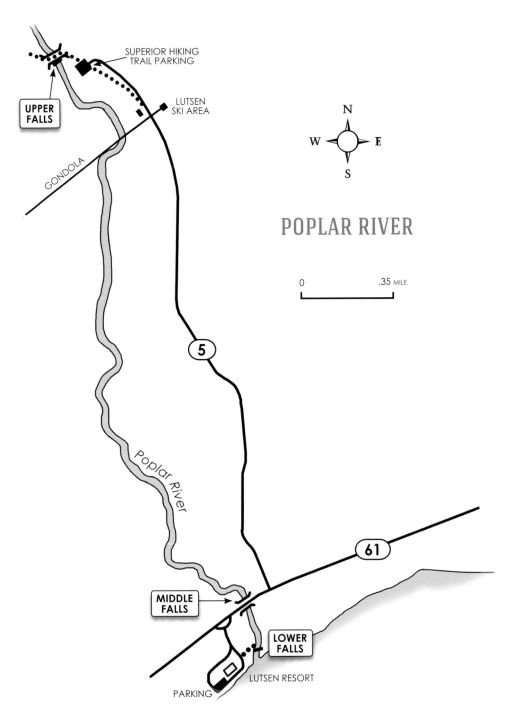

SUPERIOR HIKING
TRAIL PARKING

LUTSEN
SKI AREA

UPPER
FALLS

GONDOLA

N
W — E
S

POPLAR RIVER

0   .35 MILE

5

Poplar River

61

MIDDLE
FALLS

LOWER
FALLS

PARKING

LUTSEN RESORT

under the bridge and on under Highway 61. It's difficult to get a view of the rest of this waterfall, though, because there is really nowhere to view it. So, the footbridge view will have to remain a teaser of what lies below.

Lower Falls at Lutsen Resort

Lower Falls

TRAILHEAD: The lower fall of the Poplar River is visible from the grounds of Lutsen Resort, the historic and scenic lodge and restaurant overlooking Lake Superior. Look for the resort's tall brick-colored wooden signpost on Highway 61 near mile marker 90. Turn in at Resort Road. Follow the one-way road around the lodge and park on the east side of the building. The river is just below the parking lot. "River Trail" is marked by a sign at the northeast end of the parking lot.

HIKE DIFFICULTY
Easy
TRAIL QUALITY
Good
ROUND TRIP
< 0.1 mile
THE EXPERIENCE
★ ★

Two lovely covered wooden bridges span the Poplar River on Lutsen Resort's grounds. One is located at the mouth of the river and the other crosses the falls. It is a short walk from the parking lot down a small dirt path and 10 concrete steps to the falls bridge, which provides a snug and rustic roost for viewing the falls. The river drops about 15 feet over a sliding falls, which runs for approximately 50 feet. The concrete structure at the base of the falls once housed a water-powered turbine that provided the first source of electricity for the resort and nearby homes.

119

Cascade Falls

CASCADE RIVER
Cascade River State Park

Cascade Falls

TRAILHEAD: The Cascade River, in Cascade River State Park, is located near mile post 100, on Highway 61. Wayside parking is located on each side of the highway. The trail to the waterfalls starts on the west side of the river.

HIKE DIFFICULTY
Easy
TRAIL QUALITY
Good
ROUND TRIP
0.2 mile
THE EXPERIENCE
★ ★ ★ ★

Cascade Trail, well-marked and well-maintained, takes you through a beautiful forest of evergreen and birch. You encounter Cascade Falls not far from the parking lot. The trail leads to an overlook bound by a wooden fence. The view is picture perfect. Looking down you see the river, framed by cedar trees, emerge from a narrow black gorge, then drop 25 feet off a shelf into a rounded hole. This is one of the most photographed waterfalls on the North Shore. A two-minute hike up the trail brings you to another overlook above Cascade Falls where you can see the water plunging down below you into the pothole basin.

The Cascades

Just upriver and 47 steps from Cascade Falls overlook is a series of four to five falls, ranging from about 8 to 20 feet in height. Here the river drops, cascading in steps, through a winding, narrow gorge rimmed with evergreen trees. This is "The Cascades," one of the most beautiful sections of river on the North Shore. Hiking this segment of the trail includes lots of ups and downs on well-constructed stairways, but it is well worth the exercise. Ten minutes into the hike, you will

HIKE DIFFICULTY
Moderate
TRAIL QUALITY
Good
ROUND TRIP
0.4 mile
THE EXPERIENCE
★ ★ ★ ★

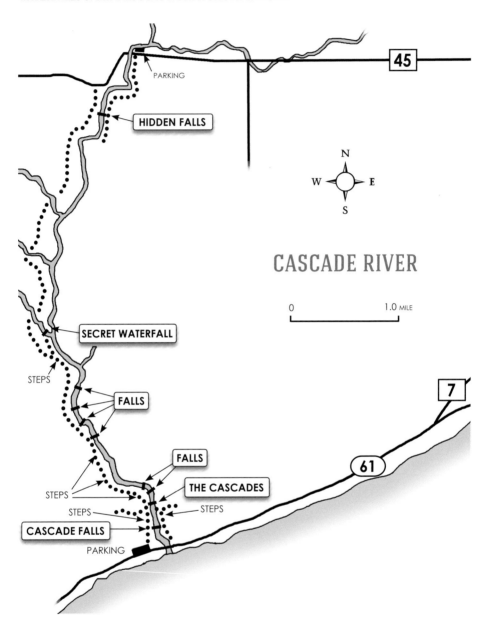

CASCADE RIVER

come to a footbridge. The overlook near the west end of the bridges affords a view of the Cascades, including one beneath the bridge. The east end of the bridge has a good view of two of the falls.

You now must decide whether to continue on the west side of the river to more falls or complete the shorter, but highly satisfying loop back downriver on the east side. Twenty-seven steps down from crossing the bridge to the east side, there is another overlook of smaller cascades. Various points along the return trail, though not formal overlooks, offer good views.

The Cascades

If you take the east side of the river loop back, be sure to glance over your shoulder periodically, so as not to miss these vistas.

More Cascade River Falls

From the footbridge, the Superior Hiking Trail continues on both sides of the river, forming a 6.8-mile loop which passes numerous falls. Unless you plan to hike the entire loop, take the west side of the river for better views of the falls. The trail also leads to a "secret" waterfall, which resides in a valley on an unnamed tributary to the Cascade. Descend the 14 stone steps from the bridge. You'll see Superior Hiking Trail and Lookout Mountain trail signs. The trail is hard-packed

HIKE DIFFICULTY
Strenuous
TRAIL QUALITY
Fair to Poor
ROUND TRIP
3.4 miles from beginning of Cascade Trail
THE EXPERIENCE
★ to ★★★

dirt, with a few roots, and offers scenic views (the overlooks have railings here) into the gorge. Occasional wood or rock steps aid your modest ascent, along with occasional longer runs of railroad tie steps.

Just two minutes beyond the bridge, from the right side of the trail, you will find stone steps curving around and down to the river. As you descend them, the lichen- and moss-encrusted rock wall hugs you close, like a passageway to a secret room. The 30 steps lead to a large, conifer-shaded outcrop with a view of cedar-covered canyon walls and an 8-foot waterfall below. Visible upriver is another, similar-sized waterfall pouring through a narrow spot in the canyon. Between these two falls you can peer into the rocky depths of a crystal-clear pool.

The main trail forks about three minutes up from the stone stairway. One tine goes down to the river and one goes left, and is labeled with the sign, "Hiking Club—Superior Hiking Trail." You can take either one, as in two minutes the forks merge. (We prefer the left, as we don't consider the river hike to be worth the extra effort. It involves 50 steps, if you have unending energy. The path leads to a pleasant place to sit among large logs beached by the Cascade River.) The trail becomes much more rocky and root-strewn, though it is still well-traveled. It wends beneath birch and conifer with various overlooks along the way.

Within about three minutes, you will encounter 26 ascending railroad tie steps. If it is late summer, the trail may be flanked by bright red-orange bunchberries. Shortly, you will see signs and a map that indicates a waterfall is 1.3 miles ahead. This is also the location of "96 Steps," as it is called, just ahead and forking to the right, while Lookout Mountain Trail continues straight ahead. Sorry, but you must go down the 96 steps. We're even more sorry that you have to go up the steps on your return trip. (But why worry about that yet?) These well-constructed wooden steps have railings and two benches on which you can rest. A few yards beyond the base of the steps, a short spur to the right overlooks the river. Stay left. The cascades are not dramatic along this stretch, but they produce a melodious acoustical background as you walk beneath the conifers on the needle-carpeted path.

About 10 minutes beyond the "96 steps," and past another run of 33 railroad tie steps, the first significant waterfall in a while (about 4 feet tall) is visible from a moss-covered promontory just to the right of the trail. Be assured that the Cascade's supply of waterfalls has not yet been exhausted. The river becomes very active along this stretch. In fact, after crossing a two-plank bridge over a wet area on the trail, you will encounter a slew of various falls, occurring every minute or two along the trail, including a slide waterfall visible from an overhanging promontory, and a cascade made up of several two-foot steps, some very accessible from the trail.

About seven minutes past the plank bridge, you can access a waterfall with a drop of about 5 feet by taking a short spur trail leading down a gradual slope to the river, your descent aided by rocks and roots. There you can sit beneath a cedar tree on a ledge jutting out over the cascade; very nice! If you decide to pause here on the hike back, be sure to take this path. You will first come upon another, more precipitous, spur trail on your return trip.

Just four minutes beyond this jewel, though the trail has deteriorated somewhat, you will meet up with another significant cataract. Be very careful, as there is a substantial cliff here. The plunge of water starts out narrow, then spreads out as it curves to the left and drops 12–15 feet going around a rock outcropping and into a pool. Get a front row view from the base of the falls. Small but satisfying cascades persist as you continue along the trail.

In another five minutes, and about a half hour beyond "96 steps," the path climbs a short, steep hill with railroad tie steps and a sign reading, "Waterfall .3 mile." After the first two stairs, take the spur to the right. The trail is very narrow, skirting a hillside, and seems to end among protruding roots along the river. Keep going. Soon the rock riverbank at your left gives way to a stream entering the river. If it is a dry season, the stream's flow may be minimal. Follow the creek bed upstream, and within two minutes you will find yourself at the base of the "secret" waterfall, which drops through a rectangular notch, and slides 10 feet down the slanted rock face into a small pool. Mosses and ferns garnish the rock walls surrounding you. If the flow is modest, the falls sounds like a spring rain.

Heading back the way you came, it takes about 30 minutes from the waterfall to the base of "96 steps." If ever the trail seems to fade away, just keep the river at your left. It's always a reassuring trail marker. Forty-five minutes after leaving the "Waterfall 0.3 mile" sign, you will be back at the footbridge, and in 10 more short minutes to the trailhead.

Tall lungwort *(sometimes called bluebell, but not to be confused with harebell, which is also occasionally called bluebell)* is one of the few true blue wildflowers found on the North Shore. Most unique is the array of colors and shades displayed by the spring wildflower as it passes through its various life stages.

Hidden Falls

HIKE DIFFICULTY
Easy

TRAIL QUALITY
Fair

ROUND TRIP
1.4 miles

THE EXPERIENCE
★ ★ ★ ★

TRAILHEAD: To reach this falls, go northeast from Highway 61 on County Road 7. The intersection is near the east end of Cascade River State Park. Go 1.9 miles up County Road 7 to County Road 44 and left (west) 0.5 mile on County Road 44 to Highway 45 (Pike Lake Road). Turn left on 45 and proceed 2.6 miles. Look for a pull-off and parking area to the right, just before the Cascade River bridge. A Superior Hiking Trail sign in the parking area indicates it is 0.3 mile to Hidden Falls.

The path leads under the bridge where you can hear and soon see the river. You will walk across stretches of rough wooden planking on the trail. The path is extremely scenic, running beneath very large old cedar trees, some leaning at dramatic angles, with tentacle-like roots grabbing the trail. Extensive trail work has occurred and fallen trees are cleared from the path, but some rough stretches remain.

Eight minutes into the hike, you'll hear Hidden Falls. A short spur trail leads to the base of the upper tier cascade. Looking upriver, you will see a run of several hundred feet tumbling at a 45-degree angle over four terraces. The river pauses here in a mossy pool bound by rock outcroppings and high canyon walls. A spit of rock and sand almost completes the full circle. A rapids runs around the spit and the river splashes over yet another fall beneath a cathedral-like cedar canopy. You can get to this fall 40 yards farther down the trail. Take a sublime seat on the rock outcrop, with the cedars above, the Cascade River rushing past, and the huge boulders that check its path.

Our visit was in a low water period, so we had a fascinating, close-up glimpse into a half dozen potholes of various sizes worn into the rock. Some were very large and filled with water as smooth as glass. Standing on the lip between two potholes was an awesome experience, as we realized that powerful currents flowed where we stood when the river was high. The currents can move massive rocks. Large, rounded boulders seemed to line and be embedded in the walls of one pothole. Others lie at the bottom of the hole. Highly polished, dark rock found on flat stretches of the river between the cascades looked like they had arrived from Pluto or some exotic place. We found this lower level of Hidden Falls most fascinating because of our personal experience with the potholes. We left reluctantly, and were back at our car in 13 minutes.

There is yet another view available of Hidden Falls. If you cross the river bridge on County Road 45 and continue 0.2 mile farther, on the left is a Superior Hiking Trail parking area. A sign shows distances to the other falls in Cascade Park. If you follow this path, you will immediately see a wooden guardrail to your left—an overlook to Hidden Falls. If you continue along the path, you will get an even better eagle's eye view of the falls. Don't get too close to the edge. The vista is a dizzying 150 feet above the river, with no rail!

Thompson Falls

TRAILHEAD: Head up County Road 4 (Caribou Trail) for 17.9 miles until you come to a T. This perpendicular road is called "The Grade" or F.R.170. Go right, re-setting your odometer. At 3.8 miles, you'll see the Eagle Mountain trailhead. Turn right at F.R.158 or Bally Creek Road. In 0.2 mile, you'll see a yellow Aquatic Management Area sign. On your right, look for a small sign nailed to a tree that says, "Thompson Falls." Park by the trailhead to your right.

HIKE DIFFICULTY
Easy
TRAIL QUALITY
Fair
ROUND TRIP
0.5 mile
THE EXPERIENCE
★ ★ ★ to ★ ★ ★ ★ ★
(if water is high)

This is a very short hike—only three minutes until the river is visible. The trail is well-trod, composed of small red stones, except for a short stretch where the stones are bigger and harder to walk on. This is also where you'll first see the calm upper stretch of the river above the waterfall. For the remaining minute or so, follow the mossy dirt trail veering left away from the river a short stretch, then right again to the waterfall. You can also continue farther downriver along a narrow, pine needle-strewn path to a small clearing with great rocks for sitting.

This cascade starts in a small pool and runs down over a black igneous rock formation that looks like a lava flow, which you can see most clearly in low water. But when high, the water itself is spectacular and rowdy. It doglegs left and then right on its 23-foot plunge over a 30-yard stretch, splitting to meander around an

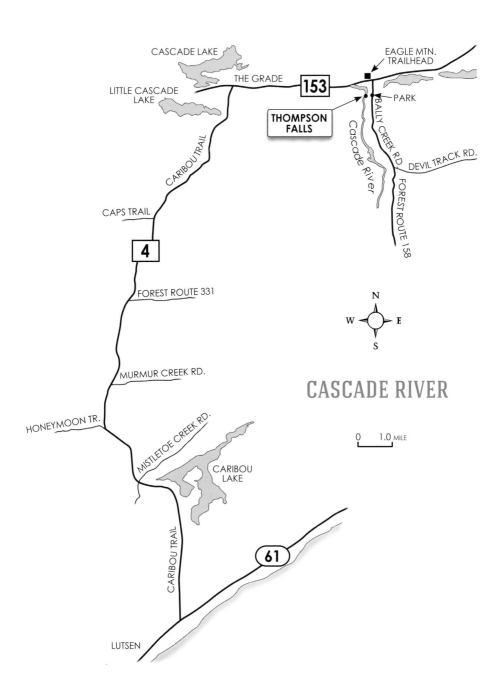

CASCADE LAKE

EAGLE MTN.
TRAILHEAD

THE GRADE

153

LITTLE CASCADE
LAKE

PARK

**THOMPSON
FALLS**

BALLY CREEK RD.

Cascade River

DEVIL TRACK RD.

CARIBOU TRAIL

FOREST ROUTE 158

CAPS TRAIL

4

FOREST ROUTE 331

MURMUR CREEK RD.

N

W   E

S

HONEYMOON TR.

MISTLETOE CREEK RD.

CASCADE RIVER

CARIBOU
LAKE

0   1.0 MILE

CARIBOU TRAIL

61

LUTSEN

Thompson Falls on the Cascade River

island complete with beautiful balsam. The topography both above and below the waterfall is relatively flat, so there's not much of a river canyon.

When heading back, be sure to stay to the left, heading upstream until you again encounter that rocky area.

The falls on Cutface Creek in spring

CUT FACE CREEK
Southwest of Grand Marais

Cutface Creek Falls

TRAILHEAD: Park at Cut Face Creek Rest Area on Highway 61, 5 miles southwest of Grand Marais and northeast of mile marker 104. Head toward the pet exercise area on the west side of the parking lot. Cross the highway to Cut Face Creek, which passes under Highway 61 west of the rest area. Your only trail is the creek bed itself. Head down a grassy embankment to the "trail."

HIKE DIFFICULTY
Easy
TRAIL QUALITY
Poor
ROUND TRIP
0.6 mile
THE EXPERIENCE
★★

There is a catch to this hike. If you want to see much water falling, you will need to wade in the creek, as there is no trail. If you do not want a wet walk, you must visit Cut Face Creek when it is virtually dry, but there will be little water falling. However even, and perhaps especially, when dry, this is a very fascinating walk. Imagine that the Red Sea has parted and you have total access to the dry seabed and see everything that you never could see when there was water. It's something like that.

You see the creek from a very interesting perspective, as if you are the creek itself, making its way through layered striations of red rock, which sometimes look like the petrified bark of a gargantuan tree. Occasionally the red rock gives way to black, and you will see areas encrusted with white mineral deposits. The geological experience of this hike, if we were rating it, would earn a higher score than the waterfall experience. The creek has many curves. About eight minutes into the hike, you will encounter three fish ladders. The creek bed has noticeably more gradient and canyon walls rise above it. When water is flowing, this is a decent-sized creek—really more of a river,

If you notice a vine creeping along the ground that resembles a narrow small-needled spruce branch, it is likely the evergreen called club moss.

131

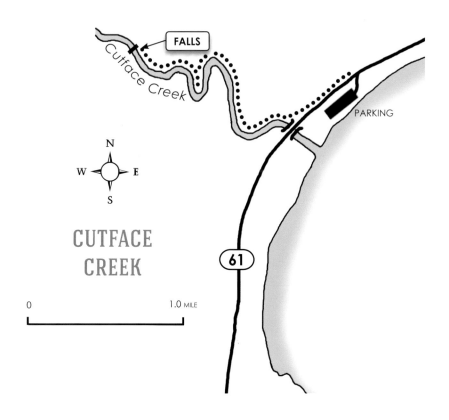

Dry creekbed of Cutface Creek

from our viewpoint. When the low-water flow is minimal, minnows hold out in some of the deeper areas between rocks.

After about 15 to 20 minutes of hiking you will come to the waterfall. *Sans* water you can closely investigate the rock structure of the long, gradual slide dropping 15 to 20 feet over a stretch of about 80 feet. Though the falls is barely wet when you can walk to it, it is wet enough to qualify as a waterfall. Diminutive cascades trickle through crannies in the waterfall bed, which is approximately 25 feet wide. You can find potholes worn when the water was wilder. Aside from the sound of the gentle water, you can experience total silence here. Find a comfortable seat and watch the graceful "water boatmen" skate across the surface of a small pool—an oasis amidst the rocks.

In the North Woods, you may come upon patches of reindeer lichen. *Only 1 to 2 inches thick, it forms cushions of tiny white branches. When dry, it is extremely brittle; when wet, it is soft. As its name suggests, it is eaten by reindeer and caribou. Woodland caribou once inhabited Minnesota's North Shore.*

Fall River Falls during high water

FALL RIVER (A.K.A. ROSEBUSH CREEK)
Southwest of Grand Marais

Fall River Falls

TRAILHEAD: This waterfall is located between Highway 61 and Lake Superior, just past mile marker 107 two miles southwest of Grand Marais. In fact, it is visible from the beach. There is no parking lot for this waterfall. We parked near the entrance to a gravel pit across the highway, about 50 yards east of the river. You can also park on the shoulder of the highway. A narrow, well-worn path leads through birch and balsam on the east side of the river.

HIKE DIFFICULTY
Moderate
TRAIL QUALITY
Poor
ROUND TRIP
0.2 mile
THE EXPERIENCE
★ ★ ★

Depending on water and wind conditions, you will either hear the sound of the surf or the sound of the falls. Two minutes from the highway you will find an overlook of Fall River Falls. The 30-foot cataract pitches over the rough rock face, flanked by patches of orange lichen. Water flow here can vary wildly. In May or early June, after lots of rain, the falls really should earn another star in

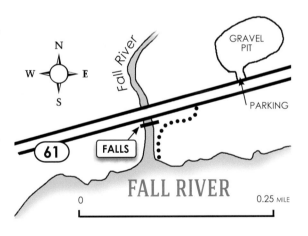

our rating system. Later, in August, you would hardly recognize it as the same place. From the spit of land in front of the falls (or perched on a rock ledge in the spring), the scene is framed by 45-degree slanting rocks. The water plunges into a pool then makes a short run across the beach. The beach is lovely, with basalt rocks jutting out into the surf and the roar of the waterfall behind you.

Barrier Falls

DEVIL TRACK RIVER
Northeast of Grand Marais

Three encounters with Barrier Falls

The first attempt: autumn almost...

TRAILHEAD: The Devil Track River is located approximately 4 miles past Grand Marais on Highway 61. Parking is along the highway, with no parking allowed on the bridge.

HIKE DIFFICULTY
Strenuous

TRAIL QUALITY
No trail

ROUND TRIP
No trail

THE EXPERIENCE
★ ★

Be forewarned. There is no trail at river level on Devil Track River. If you want to stay at water level, the trail is, literally, the river itself. If you are up for an adventure, if it is a dry time of the year and the water is low, if it is warm enough that you don't mind the cold water, if you have shoes you don't mind getting wet, if you are prepared to get wet well up to your thighs (if you are fortunate enough not to slip and fall, that is), if you are prepared to watch every step you take, if you are not alone and one of you can go get help if your companion falls and breaks an extremity, and if you have at least three-and-a-half hours to invest in this adventure, then the Devil Track may be for you.

We embarked on this adventure during a late summer drought. There were a few short stretches where we could walk on dry land—sandbars in the river, several yards of path along the river. But the vast majority of the hike, even in a dry year, is balancing on rocks mid-river and actually wading in the water. Submerged rocks are extremely slippery. There are also sections of smooth rock outcrop that are even

Formerly called by the Ojibwe, *"Manido bimadagako-wini-zibi"* or "The Spirits Walking Place on the Ice River," today's name of Devil Track River may have referred to its many cascades, which made log driving down the river extremely difficult.

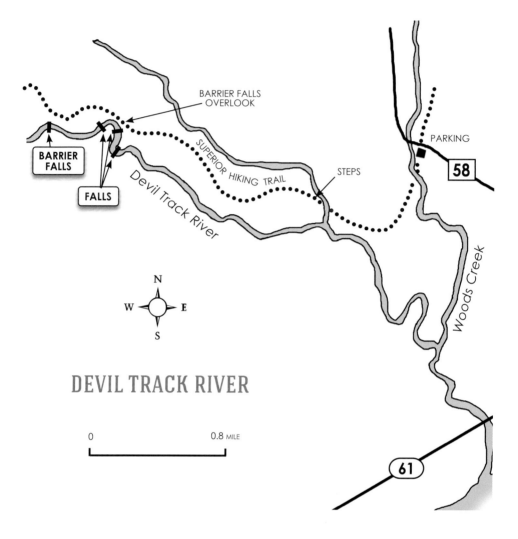

BARRIER FALLS
OVERLOOK

SUPERIOR HIKING TRAIL

PARKING

STEPS

58

BARRIER
FALLS

FALLS

Devil Track River

Woods Creek

N
W E
S

DEVIL TRACK RIVER

0   0.8 MILE

61

more slippery. Some of the most stable-looking rocks actually wobble when stepped on. In short, you can trust no place you step. We developed a technique. Walking on submerged stretches of rhyolite shards offered us the most traction and peace of mind. We traversed back and forth across the river, picking out the least intimidating crossings. The going was slow and necessitated some backtracking, as we realized there was, perhaps, a better place to cross 20 yards back.

About one hour into the hike, red canyon walls began to rise around us. Pieces of the rock wall have splintered off and fallen, resembling stacks of playing cards, but sharp as knives. The river began to wind more tightly. Gold signs designating the area as fish sanctuary appeared on both sides of the river. One hour and 20 minutes into the hike, we encountered a small waterfall that marks the beginning of a series of such cascades, occurring at five-minute intervals, and marked by water that looks like a moving veil of lace covering the gorgeous red river bed. The canyon walls get higher, rising several hundred vertical feet. The zigzagging of the river increases the drama as the canyon continues to rise. Around each turn we found yet another cascade, as well as more signs designating the fish sanctuary. The crossings to get to the next falls became trickier, with a smooth bedrock river bed. We actually felt most stable on all fours.

An enchanting encounter on the way to Barrier Falls

Barrier Falls is located about two hours into the trek, five minutes past where the river takes yet another turn to a waterfall about 15 feet high, which we found to be impassible. The river takes a 90-degree turn to the right, flowing in steps down two smaller cascades, and making another right-hand turn, so that it seems to head back in the very direction from which it came. It was getting darker and colder down in that deep, deep canyon, and we didn't know, then, how close or how far we were from Barrier Falls. So we made a decision—declare that this must be Barrier Falls, because it sure was a barrier to us—or conclude that we had just spent two hours in a fruitless attempt to see a waterfall which probably was just around the next bend. We had a long walk ahead to get back to our car before dark. We settled for the former, and lived with that fiction until about nine months later, when a DNR expert told us that if we had indeed reached Barrier Falls on that day, we would have no doubts about it. But we didn't know that then.

We headed back and an hour and a half later, we emerged from the river feeling as though we had just spent three-and-a-half hours on horseback—our leg muscles were exhausted from ankle to thigh. The unending vigilance required for each step on the journey was taxing. That vigilance had been enhanced by several very close calls, a sprained wrist, and an encounter with a young couple heading upriver as we were heading back. The young man said, "This is just about the spot where my mother slipped and broke her ankle. It took four hours to get her out."

The second attempt: summer from afar...

HIKE DIFFICULTY
Strenuous
TRAIL QUALITY
Poor
ROUND TRIP
2 miles
THE EXPERIENCE
★ ★ ★

TRAILHEAD: Turn north off of Highway 61 on Cook County Road 58. Follow County Road 58 for 0.2 mile and the road forks. Go left on Lindskog Road for 0.2 mile and turn left into the Superior Hiking Trail parking area. Signs on both sides of the road mark the trailhead. From the parking area, a sign marks the beginning of the trail to Barrier Falls, and says that it is 2.3 miles to the bridge, which is farther than you will hike to see the waterfall.

Follow the dirt path, which parallels small Woods Creek for a short distance and then veers away. You will come to seven railroad tie steps and then a wooden plank footbridge across another small creek. Six minutes from starting out, the path turns right, heading above the creek through birch and pine forest. Soon you will descend eight steps. One minute after that, you will encounter a striking mini chasm with water falling in multiple steps, splitting into several streams traversing mossy rocks. A wooden bridge crossing this stream and waterfall is just ahead, from which you can view the 8-foot plunge. Linger here awhile.

Take a hard left just after you cross the bridge. The trail then winds right and uphill, away from the stream. Rocks and roots in the path are cushioned by a carpet of pine needles. Thimbleberry (the leaves look like maple leaves) grows profusely in places. The climb continues with 26 railroad tie steps . . . and then some more steps. You may hear Devil Track River way down below. An old wooden post on the left side of the trail indicates the location of a 1937 pine plantation. Several short spur trails lead to perilous canyon overlooks. About 25 minutes into your hike, the main trail takes a dip and then rises along the ridge. Three minutes later you will see a sign for Barrier Falls Overlook.

If you are like us, you will peer into the canyon, walk back and forth, walk far-ther up the trail, peer into the canyon again, and after 10 minutes of this, finally conclude that there is no Barrier Falls and that the overlook sign really means the hike "overlooks" the fact that there is no view of Barrier Falls. But we'll clue you in. Go back about 25 feet before the overlook sign and look to the right. Raise your eyes from the bottom of the canyon to about half way between the bottom and the distant treetops–about a quarter mile away as the crow flies—and there is Barrier Falls! Sorry. As much as you may want a closer look, there isn't one, short of hiking right up the river when the water is low, and you know how that turned out for us.

A 15-minute return hike brings you back to the bridge over the mini chasm with its enchanting cascade. Explorers take note: There is a way into this little grotto of ferns and mosses. Near the base of the bridge (on the parking lot side) you'll find natural stairs of roots and rocks descending to the creek. The waterfall tumbles over multiple tiers in this peaceful paradise. We were thoroughly charmed by this little glen. The waterfall experience was much more satisfying than seeing Barrier Falls from afar. After a lengthy interlude, we hiked back to our car in nine minutes.

The third encounter: winter success!

We heard that a certain breed of humans, with whom we can find nothing in common, ski up the Devil Track River to ice climb the frozen Barrier Falls in the winter. On an early March foray up The Shore for some cross-country skiing (easy trails, please), we remembered the tales and thought we'd look to see if there were any human tracks upon the frozen river. We even entertained the remote possibility of attempting such an adventure ourselves (minus the ice climbing).

HIKE DIFFICULTY
Moderate
TRAIL QUALITY
Snow, Ice, Open Water
ROUND TRIP
2 miles
THE EXPERIENCE
★ ★ ★ ★

Looking at the Devil Track from Highway 61, we saw lots of animal tracks, but it took awhile to discern a snow-packed path—not ski tracks—heading up the frozen river. Seeing the surprising and uncharacteristic look of daring in each other's eyes, we pulled our skis out of the car, declaring, "We live on the edge!"

Skis on, we found the going easy along the well-traveled alleyway of the frozen river, but were puzzled by the lack of ski tracks. The distinctive circular marks of what we took to be ski poles on either side of the path led us to conclude this was a popular route. We agreed the river route beat any cross-country ski trail we may have chosen. The unique experience of gliding between beautiful red canyon walls that rose higher and higher, framing the white snow covering the stifled Devil Track, was exquisite. Occasional pockets of open water provided an exciting and melodic contrast.

As we continued our adventure, we noticed a phenomenon we had never seen before—"cinnamon buns" made of snow—some lying on their sides, as though displayed in a bakery window, and some standing up on end. What the heck? Some even appeared to be sprinkled with cinnamon—the rusty red sand from the canyon walls having sifted down upon them. Our analysis of these strange little formations lying at the base of the steep, snow-stuccoed rock walls led us to form our own hypothesis. We concluded that, unlike regular balls of snow that form by rolling down gradual slopes, small pieces of ice must have rolled with such velocity down the almost-vertical canyon walls, that the layers of snow had wrapped around them in one direction only. This must have produced the weird little disks that looked, to us, like cinnamon buns.

The way gradually became more difficult, as the river made tighter turns and areas of open water became more difficult to get around. Small, but nevertheless precarious-looking crevices suggested spring thaw might be closer than we thought. Though the water was shallow, we began a "what if" discussion—enjoying, as we often do, scaring ourselves with various possibilities of survival emergencies in the great wild north country. However, the packed down areas seemed solid, though wandering even inches off the path yielded soft snow in which our ski poles sank to half their length.

While negotiating a tree that had fallen thigh-high over the path—a comic scene worthy of a Lucille Ball episode—we heard human voices and saw a party of three coming up behind, sporting snowshoes and poles. Aha! That explained the tramped down sidewalk-like track and the circular prints—we never realized some snowshoers use poles. We had wondered how whoever blazed the trail had managed some of the little dips down and up, because a cross-country ski was longer than the dip was deep.

While we perceived ourselves to be moving swiftly upriver, the trio easily passed us. The going became a bit trickier on skis. Should we just take off our skis and walk on the packed path? We were tired of getting in and out of our ski bindings for stretches where our lack of skiing skill might land us in the drink, such as on curves or where the icy surface slanted toward open water. But our theory that the distribution of our weight on skis made us less likely to break through the ice, should it prove thinner than it appeared, convinced us to labor on. Soon a final, especially sharp twist of the river, with an inadequate shoulder to ski upon, made continuing on skis impossible. So we took them off, stashed them beside the trail, and trekked on foot for what proved to be only five more minutes to Barrier Falls.

Muffled by snow and ice, the roar of Barrier Falls was not audible until we were upon it. The snowshoers appeared to have arrived well ahead of us, and the male in the party remarked that they had already scaled the waterfall and come back down. My jaw dropped until I realized I had been taken, and we all had a good guffaw at my expense.

Barrier Falls in winter is an awesome, 25-foot-tall confection of ice and snow reminiscent of some wild and crazy rock formation right out of Carlsbad Caverns. A large, gleaming protuberance bulges from the center, indicating, perhaps, a boulder that projects when the cascade is fluid. Winter hid the waterfall's power from us, but we had a glimpse of the reality beneath the ice. An opening at the base of the falls was a window into the hidden torrent. The rush of water was not constant, as one might expect, but rather reminded us of the Lake Superior surf—forces alive and violent battled beneath the ice.

The chill air shortened our lingering time at Barrier Falls, making the success of our third attempt to get close to the waterfall somewhat anticlimactic. We took advantage of our exercise-heated bodies as long as we could before reluctantly turning back. Though we thought the return walk and ski took no more than half an hour, it actually took almost twice that long even though the gentle descent of the river made skiing virtually effortless. On the return trip, we passed a gentleman on foot—not even wearing snowshoes—and another party on skis. On an otherwise quiet, winter Sunday afternoon on the Shore, it was obvious that the Devil Track is a well-known and popular winter path.

Kadunce River

KADUNCE RIVER
Colvill

Kadunce River Falls

TRAILHEAD: The Kadunce River is in the town of Colvill near milepost 118. Parking is located on the lake side of Highway 61. Walk across 61 to the trailhead on the east bank, where a sign reads "Spur Trail for Superior Hiking Trail."

HIKE DIFFICULTY
Moderate
TRAIL QUALITY
Fair
ROUND TRIP
2 miles
THE EXPERIENCE
★ to ★★★★

Interestingly, Kadunce wasn't the original name for this waterway. In the 1850s it was called the Diarrhea River for reasons we really don't want to contemplate. The sign at the trailhead indicates that it is 0.9 mile to Kadunce bridge. The path starts as a wide, well-packed dirt trail. You will almost immediately see a series of small, 1-foot man-made waterfalls built to help the fish make their way upstream. A conifer and birch forest surrounds you. The Kadunce serenades you as the trail rises above the river and canyon walls begin to form. Five minutes into the hike, you will come upon 40 steps taking you above the river level. Next comes an overlook into the canyon, with a cave visible on the opposite wall. The canyon is so deep and narrow that a sign warns you not to throw rocks into the abyss, perhaps injuring someone unseen below. Keep ascending.

In two minutes you will hear a cascade. The trail rises and gently curves to the left. Just as the path begins to turn right you will notice a 10-foot path backtracking to your left. It leads to a nice view of a waterfall. If you have never considered yourself a "tree-hugger" before, become one now. Hugging trees may save your life. These canyon walls are steep, and it's a long way down. This waterfall is engaging; a secret,

Once you have spotted the diminutive star flower, *you will always recognize this denizen of the verdant miniature ecosystems on the forest floor. Often making its home among forest mosses, each tiny hair-thin stem of the star flower holds a vortex of small pointed leaves above which projects a tiny white star-shaped bloom.*

145

almost hidden, waterfall pouring into a little cave where the river takes a 180-degree turn around a canyon headland. Continue on the main path and when the trail comes to a T you can go right (upriver) or hard left, on a short spur loop through the pines for another waterfall view. This path is cushiony with moss, and the little beak of land on the canyon rim is host to diminutive northland plants and flowers. Stay close to the canyon edge and you will soon glimpse the falls below. The view of the falls is somewhat obstructed, due to conifers and the height of the canyon walls.

Continue following the main trail upriver. You may hear tumbling water down below, but if you try looking into the canyon you won't see anything. After about six minutes you will pass a cleared area on the left side of the trail. You should hear the sounds of a pretty good-sized waterfall—one you can actually see this time. Walk one more minute and there is another overlook at the top of the falls. The canyon here is only about 15 feet across. In our humble opinion, this is the best waterfall on the Kadunce, at least four stars. The water emerges from a dark, narrow canyon, passing through a fissure only 2 or 3 feet wide. It takes a steep, 12-foot slide into a horseshoe-shaped basin. The walls of the canyon and rocks beneath the falls are a natural study in black and red. The river curves left, makes another drop, curves again, and drops once more, finally burrowing down into the dark, shadowy depths of the canyon. We call this magical place "Heart of the Earth Falls."

Heart of the Earth Falls

Moving on upriver, you come to another smaller waterfall after only a minute of walking. It is a gradual, fleecy slide flowing down and around a corner. Look closely. If the water flow isn't too strong, you can see the black- and red-patterned rock looking like a giant snakeskin beneath the water. Right after this falls, you return to the river level again. We're not sure how that happens, since we were distracted by all the waterfalls.

The well-worn trail continues along the river. Around the next bend is a small 3-foot fall. A bridge and bench are located just above the top of this slide, now half an hour into your hike. If you want to see some more small falls, cross the bridge. About 100 yards past the bridge, the Superior Hiking Trail continues off to the left and uphill. The river trail continues as a smaller, informal path through the woods. You will shortly find a long curving slide of shallow water with moss lining both sides of its course. The narrow trail continues on and heads away from the river for a short distance. When it brings you back to the river, look upstream and you will see a shallow waterfall slipping over 2- to 4-foot rounded shelves as it drops a total of 12 feet before heading into a small pool. Notice that maple trees have been added to the forest canopy as the trail takes a final curve and ends. With no lollygagging it took us 20 minutes to walk from the bridge back to our car.

Devil's Kettle

BRULE RIVER

Judge C.R. Magney State Park

Brule River Falls

TRAILHEAD: The Brule River is located in Judge C. R. Magney State Park 14 miles northeast of Grand Marais on Highway 61 near milepost 124. Approaching from the west, turn left into the park, pass the ranger station and proceed 0.2 mile to the parking lot. On the lot's east end is a sign informing you that it is 1 mile to the Devil's Kettle. Follow this trail to Upper Falls, Devil's Kettle, and more.

HIKE DIFFICULTY
Strenuous
TRAIL QUALITY
Good to Fair
ROUND TRIP
2 miles to Devil's Kettle Falls
THE EXPERIENCE
Upper Falls ★ ★ ★ to ★ ★ ★ ★ depending on how high the water is.
Devil's Kettle Falls ★ ★ ★ ★

The trail begins with well-groomed gravel and easy walking. You cross a footbridge over a small stream, and then soon come to another footbridge crossing the river over a small, unnamed waterfall. On the east bank the trail turns upstream and begins to rise, offering a beautiful view of the big river below (now on your left). About 17 minutes into your hike, the trail is still wide and clear. You will see more falls as the mighty Brule meanders through the canyon. Less than 10 minutes later, you will reach a T in the path and a posted map. Take a left at the T, and you'll find a bench with a panoramic view of distant Upper Falls. Take a break and enjoy it. Continue on the main trail, going right. You will encounter steps—lots of steps.

We counted 167 leading down to a ramp and then more wooden steps. Gravity is your friend on the way down to the Devil's Kettle. Appreciate it while you can. At the bottom you'll pass an unmarked flight of 21 metal stairs heading left, down to the river and upper falls. After viewing the Kettle, be sure to explore this path. Eight minutes beyond the T, the trail becomes rougher. A sign directs you to overlooks of

---

The Brule River *has also been called Arrowhead River and Burnt Wood River. The French word, "Bruler" means "to burn." The Ojibwe name was "Wisakode-zibe"—"Half Burned Wood River," likely a testimony to forest fire.*

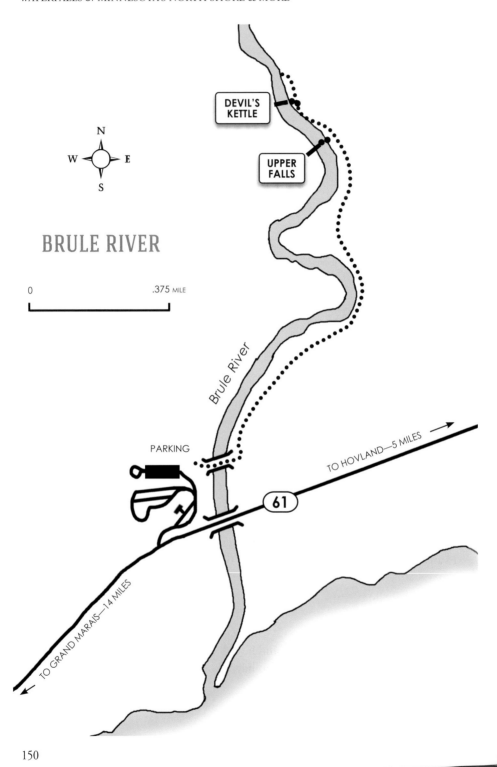

N
W • E
S

BRULE RIVER

DEVIL'S
KETTLE

UPPER
FALLS

Brule River

0   .375 MILE

PARKING

TO HOVLAND—5 MILES

61

TO GRAND MARAIS—14 MILES

Devil's Kettle Falls. Two over-looks provide different views of Devil's Kettle. You can look into the Kettle from the second overlook, if you stand in the far left corner of the platform. Note the lush moss upholstering the steep rock walls all the way to the water's edge. The right half of the Devil's Kettle Falls plummets into a narrow oval basin and runs a short course through the canyon to the Upper Falls. The mysterious left half plunges into a hole and no one really knows where it emerges. There is plenty of Devil's Kettle lore. The strangest tale we've heard is that a car was pushed into the hole and never resurfaced. The part we don't get is how anyone could get a car up there to begin with, let alone push it into the river? We do believe the stories that researchers have dropped ping-pong balls and dye into the hole. But a car… we don't think so. Its a strange tale, but the Devil's Kettle is a strange place.

Upper Falls

Now that you've seen the main attraction, head back to the metal stairs. We know you're tired from trudging down all the stairs, and your calf muscles may be in spasm in anticipation of the climb back up, but believe us, the extremely short side trip to Upper Falls is well worth it.

On the last leg of the trail to Devil's Kettle, 22 metal steps lead you to the base of awesome Upper Falls. Narrow on top, the fall broadens in a powerful torrent as it pours water 25 to 30 feet over a series of steep steps, producing billowing clouds of mist and spray that highlight the rusty brown hues of its rocky foundation. Devil's Kettle is impressive, but Upper Falls offers a more intimate, and in some ways more satisfying, waterfall experience. The enchanting falls are close and big, the water is fat (yes, its looks fat), and huge bubbles the size of volleyballs bob by on the turbulent current. Rest here. You have lots of steps to climb on the return trip.

High Falls

PIGEON RIVER
Grand Portage State Park

Pigeon River Falls

Grand Portage State Park is unique. Historically, the Pigeon River was an important travel route for indigenous people and fur traders. The park is located at the farthest eastern reaches of Minnesota, and the Michigan border is just off shore in Lake Superior. This is the only state park not owned by the state, but rather by the Grand Portage Band of the Ojibwe, which leases it to the state. The Pigeon River (named after the extinct passenger pigeons that once frequented the area) marks the boundary between Canada and the U.S., and is also the largest river along the Minnesota portion of the North Shore. Most relevant for this book, the park contains the highest waterfall of Minnesota's North Shore.

High Falls

TRAILHEAD: Take Highway 61 to Grand Portage State Park, which is within the Grand Portage Indian Reservation. The entrance to the park is near mile marker 150, 7 miles northeast of the village of Grand Portage, just before you reach the U.S. Customs station at the Canadian border. The park entrance is just opposite the back of the "Welcome to Minnesota" sign. There is also a Grand Portage Park sign and a rest area/travel info sign. Turn left into the park, go right when the road forks, for the closest parking.

HIKE DIFFICULTY
Easy
TRAIL QUALITY
Good
ROUND TRIP
1 mile
THE EXPERIENCE
★ ★ ★ ★ ★

Access the High Falls Trail by going straight through the new visitor center, out the back door, and across a new boardwalk. Be sure to stop on your way and take in this impressive new interpretive facility, highlighted by beautiful graphics beneath your feet. Or you can just proceed to the right, around the building. The trail is excellently maintained, paved and handicapped accessible. The paved trail leads

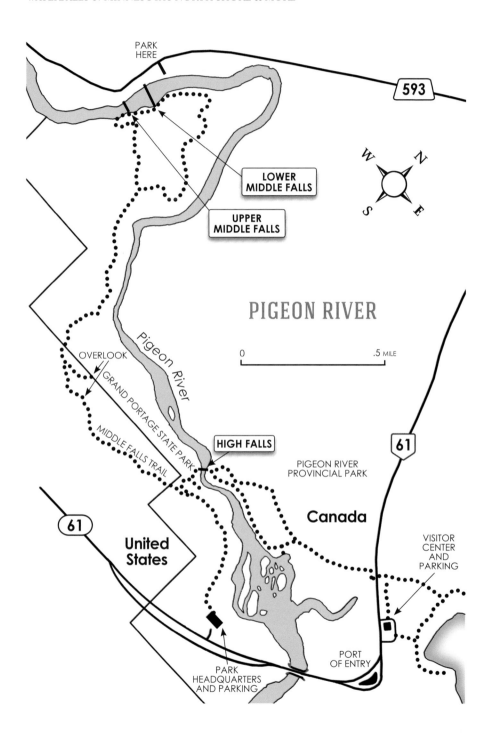

one-half mile to the High Falls. Within a minute or so of starting off, you can already hear the rumble. Birches, maples, and evergreens surround you. Interpretive signs and friendly benches mark the way. Seven minutes into the walk, the trail becomes a long boardwalk that gradually ascends a rocky ridge. The boardwalk lends a tree-house feel to the hike as it rises above the forest floor. The walkway then accesses three well-constructed wooden overlooks of the High Falls. One has a handicapped accessible ramp. The other two include modest flights of stairs. All three provide different perspectives on the spectacular High Falls.

Interpretive materials at the park say the height of Pigeon High Falls has not been officially measured, but it is estimated at 120 feet, the equivalent of a 10- to 13-story building. When the river is high, water thunders over the drop at 3,200 gallons per second. High Falls and the formidable gorge are at the lower end of a several-mile reach of rapids and falls impassable by canoe. Native Americans, and later the voyageurs, referred to this area as "The Great Carrying Place" and bypassed the stretch by hauling canoes and freight over the 8-mile Grand Portage.

The High Falls crashes down into a black rock gorge. The main torrent, joined on the left by a less voluminous cascade, pounds into a large pool and then spills over a large slide. Just downstream the river tumbles out of the gorge into a placid estuary that ends about a mile farther downstream at Lake Superior. The backdrop is awesome—forested hills rise up and surround the gorge, and the sky is as big as the water. What more can we say? You just have to see it.

Middle Falls

TRAILHEAD: If you visited High Falls first, backtrack to the outhouse you passed on High Falls Trail. The trail to Middle Falls begins there.

A sign describes the 3.6-mile hike as "rugged." Be aware that it is both rugged and strenuous. The trail begins as a gravel path winding through lovely balsam and birch forest. On the forest floor, the contrast of fallen white birch trunks among green ferns is stunning. You'll cross wooden planking and the trail soon begins to rise, and the gravel path gives way

HIKE DIFFICULTY
Strenuous
TRAIL QUALITY
Poor
ROUND TRIP
4.4 miles from parking lot
THE EXPERIENCE
★★★ to ★★★★★

to packed dirt and roots. Only a few feet wide in places, the trail is easily discernable. In fall, portions of the path are paved in pine needles and autumn leaves. Other trail sections are marginal, slippery and rugged. Be sure to watch your step, because the boreal beauty of moss-covered rocks and logs, colorful lichens, and mushrooms may draw your focus away from the shortcomings of the path.

Twelve minutes from the trailhead, a steeper climb begins. Steps of small logs and shale help you wind up a sharp rise. Your reward at the top is a view of Lake Superior, from a rock outcrop clad in reindeer lichen, with a convenient bench to rest upon. The trail descends once more from this promontory, and 18 minutes into your hike, you will go up a run of stone steps, flanked by a log banister. You will then encounter a path going off to the right. This path goes a short distance to another overlook. Continue straight on the main trail. You will notice numbers posted along the trail. They affirm that you are on the right path.

About 20 minutes into the hike, you will hear what sounds like another falls. There is no easy way to see what's there, so keep going. The trail climbs and descends, and the pathway is slick in places. The sound of white water comes and goes, but about 30 minutes into your adventure, it gets much louder. In another seven minutes, you reach a fork going off to the right. This path is a loop along the river bank. We were told that it is often wet, though new paths bypass the muddy section. Stay left. Forty-five minutes from beginning Middle Falls Trail, you will step out upon a rock outcropping at the upper portion of Middle Falls.

Upper Middle Falls, as we call it, emerges from a wide, calm, almost lake-like portion of the river, with a backdrop of towering birch and aspen. It pitches over a 10-foot chute, creating an explosion of white water. Linger on the flat basalt outcrop edging the falls. See if you can find the linear white quartz intrusions crossing the black rock. Looking down river from Upper Middle Falls, you will see that the river disappears over another drop-off. The best part of Middle Falls is yet to come.

Go back to the path and head a few hundred yards downriver to find one of our favorite falls on The Shore. Though its fame is eclipsed by High Falls, the Lower Middle Falls made us glad we decided to explore the Pigeon River. The strenuous hike to get there was worth the effort.

You can view Lower Middle Falls from several different angles. It is possible to see it from above, where close inspection of the crumbly black rock reveals thousands of tiny waterfalls. Viewed from the side, it is framed by towering evergreens and aspen. Or it can be seen head-on, from a black rock spit that juts out below the falls. Each perspective is gorgeous. We estimate the falls to be 20 feet high.

The river enters the main chute from three directions, forming a vee of water that crashes head-on at the bottom of the falls. The mist produced by this turbulence can rise to the tops of the trees, creating ideal conditions for rainbows, depending upon the cooperation of the sun. Another, smaller section of the falls comes down on the right. Below the falls the river runs wide and calm.

To head back the way you came, go to the path and turn right. Twenty-seven minutes of walking brought us back to the bench and the plank walkway. Forty-one minutes from Middle Falls, we reached the trailhead and outhouse. Ten minutes more and we were back at the visitor center. *Note: For a photo, as well as an easier way to view the falls, see p. 165.*

Partridge Falls

TRAILHEAD: Partridge Falls is located on the Grand Portage Indian Reservation. Going northeast on Highway 61, 24.8 miles northeast of Grand Marais, turn left onto County Road 17/89 (Old Highway 61). Take this for 6.3 miles where it intersects at a T with County Road 17/Mineral Center Road. Turn left and continue on County Road 89 for two miles. You will then turn left onto Partridge Falls Road, which is marked with a green road sign on the left. (This is a dirt road, not in the best condition.) The road forks at 2.9 miles but stay left. Go another 1.3 miles and you will come to the Pigeon River. Park here. The trail to the Partridge Falls is to your right heading downriver.

HIKE DIFFICULTY
Moderate
TRAIL QUALITY
Fair
ROUND TRIP
0.2 mile
THE EXPERIENCE
★ ★ ★ ★ ★

Partridge Falls Road is much improved over what we encountered while writing the first edition of this book, although there are still a few rough spots. But the road is still panoramic. Abundant, lavender-colored fireweed lines the narrow road in July and August. You are in the midst of wilderness.

Partridge Falls is at the end of the road at a dirt turnaround beside the Pigeon River. Leave your car and head right downstream. You will find a grassy trail that soon becomes well-packed dirt. The trail quality is poor. You must step over gnarled and tangled roots that seem to be conspiring to make the going difficult.

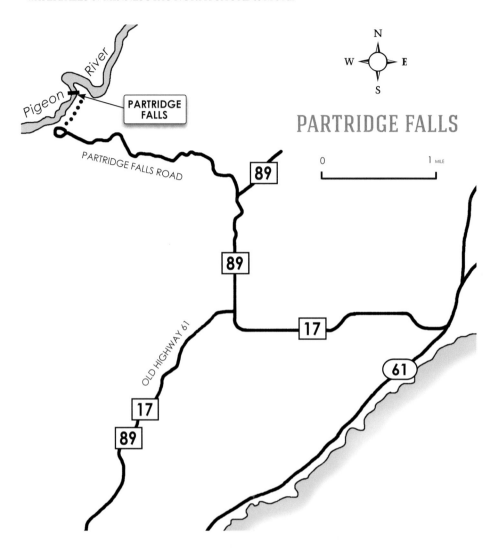

PARTRIDGE FALLS

Three minutes into the hike, you will hear the rumble of the nearby falls. One more minute brings you to a cleared area with shale outcrops offering a precarious overlook of something really, really big. You can't get the best look from here. The path continues either downriver or down the bank to the river. The river path will not get you a better view of the falls, because the river hooks to the right. Instead, go left and make your way directly, but very carefully, downhill to the river on the needle-strewn rock, root, and dirt "path." The way is short, but very steep. You pass through a narrow ravine where an immense, mossy rock wall seems like a huge dam holding back the falls. You can better appreciate this perspective on your way back up.

Partridge Falls is jaw-dropping awesome! A huge 30-foot mountain of exploding white froth from bank to bank, the waterfall definitely ranks as one of the big boys of the North Shore. You can stand on rock outcrops within 10 feet of the base of this thundering monster with mist roiling off the bottom like smoke from a dragon. Partridge Falls puffs out its chest—the frothing water bulges out—as if it is not enough just to tower and bellow above you. Because of this unusual shape, it is possible to see falls behind falls—beneath the outer sheet of water you can see other falls in another layer spilling down the boulders behind.

Partridge Falls

How is it possible that, after all this, the creature's surging power is then wedged through a 4-foot notch just downriver from the dragon's black den? Light green moss and a few brave plants manage to hang on in this canyon melee; dark rock walls rise vertically up above you, topped with tenacious conifers. Notice the 2 1/2-foot diameter pine trunks strewn to the left of the base of the falls, like the bones of some mammoth beast that ventured too close to the dragon.

Heading back, enjoy the beautiful setting of the steep ravine path even as you search for root handholds and rock footholds. If you are as lucky as we were, a soaring hawk may escort you on the bouncing, 20-minute drive from Partridge Falls back to the intersection of Partridge Falls Road and Old Highway 61. Don't forget to watch for rocks and holes. It could be a very long walk back to "civilization!"

Ontario Waterfalls

Most people visiting the North Shore might not even consider a day trip into Canada, especially just to see waterfalls. But if you're reading this book, you should. Ontario has much to offer in the way of waterfalls, as you'll see in this section.

The first thing you might wonder about is whether it's a hassle to make the border crossing. Well it takes a bit more planning than it used to. The crossing at the Pigeon River International Bridge is open 24 hours a day, seven days a week, year round. Every year, over a half-million Americans cross from Minnesota into Canada at seven different points along the border, so you can, too (See Crossing Into Canada, page 185).

After that, the transition into Canada is easy. Minnesota Highway 61 becomes Ontario Highway 61 all the way to Thunder Bay. Mileage signs change to kilometer signs, so don't be confused if sites suddenly seem farther away than they really are. Multiply kilometers by .6. As in 1 kilometer is six-tenths of a mile. Or 60 kilometers is 36 miles. Or 100 kilometers is 60 miles. We chose the intersection of the two major highways in Thunder Bay as the navigational hub from which to direct you to the waterfalls. That point is located roughly 42 miles (or 70 kilometers) north of the U.S. border, taking Highway 61 (a.k.a. Thunder Bay Expressway). The Trans-Canadian Highway (also called Highway 11/17) runs east/west through Thunder Bay. Our directions are gauged in miles, so if you're from the U.S., like us, you can go by your odometer. An interesting tidbit is that Thunder Bay sits astride the geographical center line of Canada.

CANADA

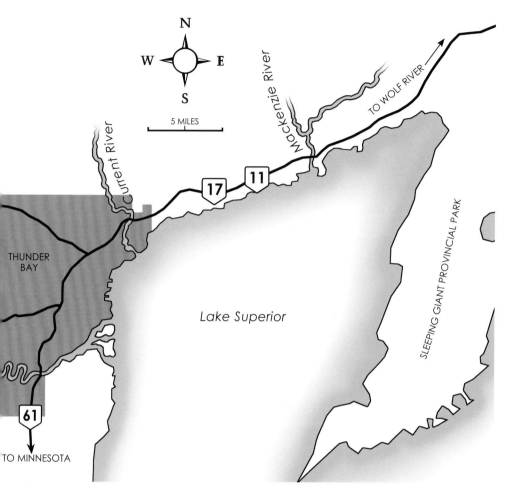

As for waterfalls, you'll find many in the vicinity—a study in contrasts. Some waterfalls splash in developed Thunder Bay parks, some thunder in Canadian provincial parks, and some cascade in undeveloped areas that feel mighty remote. Those within the city are fairly modest. Visit them only if you have time after seeing Kakabeka Falls in the provincial park of the same name, about 17 miles from Thunder Bay. Another must-see (for the more adventurous) is Dog Falls in Silver Falls Provincial Park. Don't let the fact that it's located in one of Ontario's counterparts to our state parks fool you, though. This isn't like any state park we've ever visited before—even compared to our own pretty primitive Crosby Manitou State Park. Read the directions to all of these Ontario waterfalls before you decide.

High Falls from the Canadian side of Pigeon River

PIGEON RIVER
Pigeon River Provincial Park

High Falls

TRAILHEAD: Immediately (0.1 mile) after crossing the Canadian border you'll see, on your right, the Ontario Travel Information Center. The hike to the High Falls begins at the north end of this parking lot. (See corresponding map on page 154 for Waterfalls of Pigeon River on the Minnesota side.)

HIKE DIFFICULTY
Moderate
to Strenuous

TRAIL QUALITY
Fair

ROUND TRIP
2.5 miles

THE EXPERIENCE
★ ★ ★ ★ ★

New signage and an artistic gateway mark the obvious beginning of the trail to the High Falls, with handsome brick steps and a handicapped accessible ramp followed by an impressive boardwalk. Less than a minute into following the boardwalk, you will encounter a large interpretive sign for the park. Accessibility ends here, as you head left onto a dirt trail.

This narrow trail winds through balsam forest where many boreal woodland plants thrive. Scattered boardwalks span muddy areas. Four minutes into the hike we noticed an especially sumptuous bed of moss and horsetail plant to the left of the trail. Identification of the latter will be easy for you. It is considered a living fossil, inhabiting Paleozoic forests for over 100 million years.

A couple of minutes later the trail divides, a sign indicates Finger Point Trail to the right, but you go left. Soon a small sign tells you that it is 1.5 km. to High Falls. Fourteen minutes into the hike, we encountered another boardwalk on which you head left. You'll also come to a sign indicating that it is 0.5 km. back to the Tourist Center. But continue straight on, beneath Highway 61, and then head right, on the now gravel trail. Soon the path takes a left back into the soft shade of the woods and broadens wide enough to accommodate park vehicles.

In three more minutes you'll come to a fork where you go right and see a sign that it's only 1 km. to the High Falls. The grade rises gently, then steeply. Seven minutes later, dirt gives way to rock outcrop, and you'll see a sublime vista of the Pigeon River flowage. Two minutes farther you come to a T, with a great view of the falls to the left from an official metal-railed overlook. If you go right, toward the "Danger Steep Cliffs" sign, you get a view from the top of the waterfall.

When you go left, you'll spy a very large wooden sluice—a remnant of those that, years ago, channeled logs to bypass the falls for a gentler ride downriver. The trail drops steeply to get to the sluice, which is actually part of the trail and also features interpretive signs, including a photo of the site from the 1890s. This takes you to the High Falls overlook.

The view of the High Falls is stunning as it rolls over the lip and crashes 120 feet down the steep canyon walls. You are viewing the middle main chute of the waterfall. Water level does fluctuate on the Pigeon, greatly affecting how spectacular the waterfall appears. When we visited in September, the flow was quite narrow, hitting rocks midway down the drop, then spreading out. In late July, the volume was much greater.

Delicate bell flowers and grasses tremble in the dampening breath of the falls as they cling to the fascinating textured rock by the overlook. Straight across the river you'll see one of the viewing platforms on the American side. The other is to your left. Though viewing from the Canadian side does offer a different perspective, it doesn't get you appreciably closer to the waterfall.

Leaving the falls overlook to return to the main trail loop, check out the avant-garde metal bench illustrating the sluicing of timber, a log jam, and the waterfalls. See if you can find the four loggers. Hint: It's easier to see the representations from a distance. Retrace your steps though the sluice, and rather than going back uphill the way you came, head right, down several runs of steps (totaling 62) and boardwalks.

Ten minutes post-falls, find an old chimney—ruins from a 1930s resort—after which you come to a fork in the trail and go left. Five minutes later a sign indicates 0.6 km to the tourist center. It's five more minutes to the highway bridge, then go right (not to the Finger Point Lookout trail). You'll emerge from the trail at the parking lot on the back side of the tourist center on a path lined with grayed wood two-by-fours. Our return time from High Falls to our car was 25 minutes.

The most luscious wild blueberries *are plump and dent-free. The silvery sheen on the skin protects the berry from the sun's harsh rays.*

Pigeon River Middle Falls

Middle Falls

TRAILHEAD: After crossing the U.S./Canadian border and going through customs, continue north on ON 61 for 1.6 miles. You'll see blue resort signs on the right, just before the intersection where you turn left (west) onto ON 593. After 0.9 mile, a brown log building sits to your left. Four-tenths of a mile farther, Middle Falls will appear on your left, just before a road sign indicating the road bends right. Park here.

HIKE DIFFICULTY
Easy
TRAIL QUALITY
Good
ROUND TRIP
< 0.1 mile
THE EXPERIENCE
★ ★ ★ ★

Make your way along the ruins of blacktop and slate past the old foundation footprint of a building. You'll get a lovely view of the same waterfall that requires a somewhat challenging hike on the U.S. side of the Pigeon (for details, see corresponding chapter and map for Waterfalls of the Pigeon River on the Minnesota side).

165

Stepped Trowbridge Falls

CURRENT RIVER
Kinsmen Park, Thunder Bay

Trowbridge Falls

Trailhead: From the intersection of Highway 17/11 (Trans-Canadian Highway) and Highway 61 (Thunder Bay Expressway) in Thunder Bay, head northwest on Highway 11/17 for 7.4 miles. Take the Hodder Avenue exit. Turn left onto Hodder Avenue and go 0.4 miles. When you cross over the highway, Hodder Avenue becomes Copenhagen Road. Turn left onto Trowbridge Road, which enters Kinsmen Park where you enter a large parking lot.

HIKE DIFFICULTY
Easy
TRAIL QUALITY
Good
ROUND TRIP
0.8 mile
THE EXPERIENCE
★★ to ★★★

From the parking lot, walk west 200 yards across the playground field to the far end of the grass. There, head through the opening in the fence on your left and down a short run of concrete steps to river's edge.

The fractured slate of the Trowbridge is a fascinating geological sight and definitely ups our rating of this "waterfall experience." Rock shelves provide ready-made seats from which to contemplate the tumbling water. The mini-falls' voices join together in a satisfying chorus.

This is unlike the deep, sometimes intimidating canyons through which other North Shore waterfalls flow. These are friendly falls. The embankments vary from several feet to about 12 feet, with balsam, hemlock and birch crowding to the brink of the stepped-down walls.

The river's multiple angled falls create soft rippling surf at your feet. The palette contrasts are striking—black slate, green hemlock, glowing gold birch in autumn—highlighted by alabaster birch bark and ruffled water.

Male and female black bears *cannot tolerate each other's company except during breeding season.*

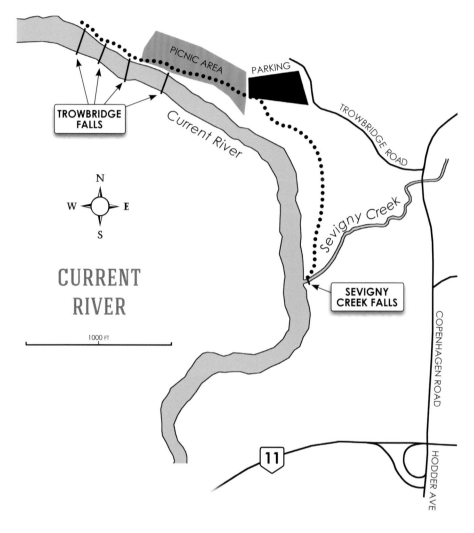

If water flow is slow to moderate, you can head upriver easily along the riverbed. If the water is high, you'll need to follow the well-trod dirt and gravel path that parallels the river, with campsites to the right of the trail.

Continue north past the suspension footbridge. This stretch of the river runs calm before more cascades appear in the upper level, and the rock becomes more free-form, wrinkly and pitted. Shiny black slate gives way to a crazy quilt of gray and rust. The total run of both upper and lower falls is approximately 400 yards.

A walk of five minutes returned us from the top of the upper cascades to the lower, then back to the playing field. Another five minutes, and we were at our car.

Sevigney Creek Falls

TRAILHEAD: Begin from the parking lot for Trowbridge Falls (see previous directions). The trail starts from the middle of the left side of the parking lot.

It's a five-minute stroll to Sevigney Creek Falls. You emerge from the trail at the edge of a shallow creek bed, between the modest upper and lower cascades. This waterfall lives where Sevigney Creek meets the Current River. The upper part of this 10-foot waterfall is narrow and comprises multiple levels. The lower falls is even prettier, though a few feet smaller. The water flows around large projecting rocks—the uppermost one looks like a mossy face in profile—and skips down several steps. When we visited at the brink of evening, we enjoyed an unexpected visit from a porcupine lumbering up a balsam tree.

HIKE DIFFICULTY
Easy
TRAIL QUALITY
Good
ROUND TRIP
0.4 mile
THE EXPERIENCE
★★ to ★★★

The Cascades

Trailhead: From the intersection of Highway 17/11 (Trans-Canadian Highway) and Highway 61 (Thunder Bay Expressway) in Thunder Bay, head northwest on Highway 11/17 for 5.1 miles and turn left onto Balsam Street, which you will take for 2.1 miles. It ends at the parking lot for the Cascades Conservation Area. The trail to the Cascades begins from the northwest end of the parking lot and starts out as the "Forest" or Green Trail.

This beautiful area of mixed deciduous and coniferous forest is within the city of Thunder Bay, where the Current River flows about 160 yards through a rock outcrop. Be sure to visit the very thorough interpretive exhibit near the parking lot. We found the aerial photo of the rock outcrop and falls area especially interesting.

HIKE DIFFICULTY
Moderate (due to walking on outcrops)
TRAIL QUALITY
Good
ROUND TRIP
1.4 miles
THE EXPERIENCE
★★★

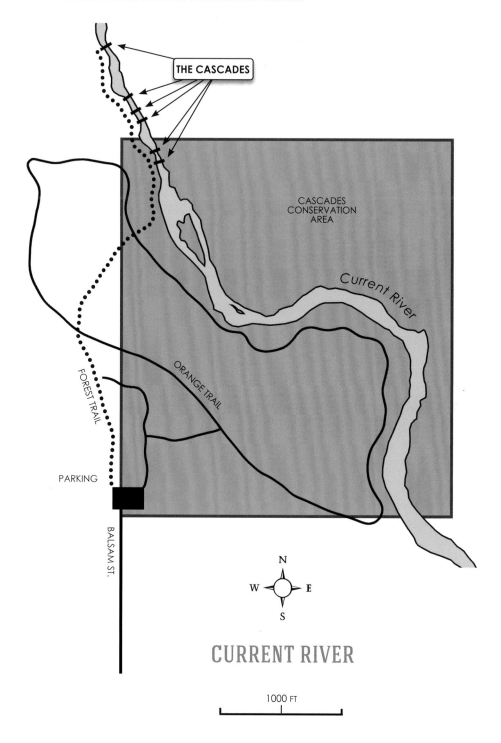

THE CASCADES

CASCADES
CONSERVATION
AREA

Current River

ORANGE TRAIL

FOREST TRAIL

PARKING

BALSAM ST.

N
W · E
S

CURRENT RIVER

1000 FT

The large network of trails can be confusing, despite maps at various locations. Unfortunately, the wheelchair accessible, paved central loop does not pass within view of the falls, though it provides a nice forest walk. But unpaved trails do branch off this loop to the falls. Don't visit here if you have a phobia of large off-leash dogs, though the many we encountered were well-behaved or too busy frolicking to pay us any attention.

The paved Forest/Green Trail intersects the wide, gravel Yellow Trail in just four minutes. Head left. Shortly the Yellow and Orange trails intersect. Continue straight on the Yellow Trail. Three minutes farther, climb 10 steps and descend 28. The trail now becomes sandy. Cross the Red Trail two minutes later. You'll soon hear the sound of the falls. Descend a short, rocky stretch to the rock outcrop that hugs the river. You'll need to cross a small stream on the well-positioned stepping stones.

Two minutes later you'll find yourself upon a huge pink outcrop stretching along the river. The rock has turned a tawny brown and black where the water has run over giant broken and tossed rock chunks. Tall pines surround the scene. If it's a hot day, expect a fair number of people lolling about on the rocks and swimming in any of multiple backwater pools.

Heading upriver (or uprock) you'll see a narrow channel of great turbulence with high stone protuberances. But don't miss what's happening right beneath your feet—rock shining like burnished copper supporting lime green lichen that resembles neon flowers. Other dainty-looking outcrop plants belie the toughness it takes to thrive in their spartan world.

This area is so popular that you'll find trails blazed everywhere, including an informal maze of them within the shady, wooded edge bordering the rock formation. Within that maze, most places where the grass (and sometimes mud) trails give way to rock usually signal a waterfall nearby, though the most straightforward journey is to just ramble along the river on the rock outcrop. The higher up you go, the fewer people you'll encounter.

Black bears *are very intelligent, with remarkable long term memory and far better navigational skills than humans.*

"Niagara of the North" — Kakabeka Falls

KAMINISTIQUIA RIVER
Kakabeka Falls Provincial Park

Kakabeka Falls

TRAILHEAD: From the intersection of Highway 17/11 (Trans-Canadian Highway) and Highway 61 (Thunder Bay Expressway) in Thunder Bay, take Highway 11/17 west for 16.8 miles. Just past the town of Kakabeka Falls, turn left into Kakabeka Falls Provincial Park. You will see the falls on the far side of the parking lot, or you can view them from the other side of the Kaministiquia River by walking or driving over the bridge just to your right.

HIKE DIFFICULTY
Easy, wheelchair accessible

TRAIL QUALITY
Good

ROUND TRIP
<0.1 mile

THE EXPERIENCE
★ ★ ★ ★ ★

You can hear the bellow of Kakabeka—Ojibwe for "thundering water on sheer cliffs"—as soon as you open your car door. This majestic cascade is sometimes referred to as "The Niagara of the North." It is the second highest waterfall in Ontario—an impressive 131 feet. Niagara is only 39 feet taller.

Kakabeka comprises two waterfalls that dive down either side of a huge shale wedge on which birch and bushes cling. Together, they span 213 feet. On the left side, the river pours over layers of shale, making for wild water as it bounces off the fractures. The larger, more voluminous right flow plunges over a cleaner edge, hitting multiple steps on its way down. The water volume fluctuates with the season, plus the dam upstream diverts varying amounts for hydroelectric power. On weekends, however, the river is unleashed, doubling its surge.

The viewing platforms for the falls are connected with an artful wooden network of boardwalks and walkways on both sides of the river, as well as along the single-lane car bridge that crosses just above the lip of the waterfall. The morning we visited, a

---

The gorge of Kakabeka Falls *hosts sensitive flora and contain some of the most ancient fossils in existence, some 1.6 billion years old.*

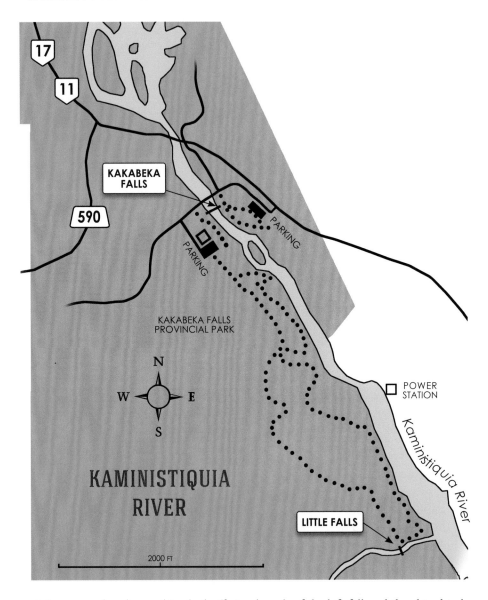

rainbow waxed and waned in the buffeting breath of the left falls, while white birch and aspen leaves quivered in the updraft from the pounding water.

The view downriver from the overlooks also is awe-inspiring, with the sparkling waters of the Kaministiquia River (Ojibwe for "meandering river with three mouths") below and pines as far as you can see. The striped canyon walls feature gray, black, and brown tones—the layers as defined as a cut onion. Candy Mountain and Knot Hill serve as backdrops to this unforgettable tableau.

Little Falls

Be sure to read the legend of the brave Ojibwe princess, Green Mantle, in the interpretive materials available in the park. Listen for the angry cries of the spectral Sioux warriors who plunged to their deaths in the cacophonous cascade. See Green Mantle's spirit, manifested as a rainbow, lingering in the mist…

Little Falls

TRAILHEAD: From the Kakabeka Falls Provincial Park Information Center, walk down river (south) to the trailhead for the Mountain Portage Walking Trail, just on the other side of a small parking area. Go straight on this trail for 600 yards, where it intersects the Little Falls Walking Trail loop. You can take this loop, either right or left, to get to Little Falls.

HIKE DIFFICULTY
Mostly easy, except for one last, steep climb
TRAIL QUALITY
Good
ROUND TRIP
2.4 miles
THE EXPERIENCE
★★★★

The path to Little Falls is a scenic mixture of deciduous and coniferous forest. It starts out on Mountain Portage Trail as crushed gravel edged with railroad ties, interesting interpretive signs and benches. Five minutes later Little Falls Trail, indicated by a marker, branches to the right. At this point the path transitions to well-trod dirt with occasional rocks and roots. On the September

175

day we trekked this trail, maples had staged their autumn transformation. Their stained glass colors combined with the stately pine spires were reminiscent of a grand Gothic cathedral.

Keep children in hand, as there is a steep drop-off, left of the trail. Thirteen minutes into our hike, the trail began to climb higher. Three minutes later we arrived at what we thought was Little Falls, in a small stream traversed by a wooden plank bridge. It certainly was little—and dry—though the steep creek bed promised a tumbling waterfall above and below the trail in wetter times.

Luckily, we decided to complete the loop and continued on an up-and-down winding passage. Moss luxuriated on each side of the trail, with bunchberry and starflower leaves indicative of the spring flora that inhabits this place.

To our surprise and pleasure, about 45 minutes into our hike, and not too far beyond what we had assumed was Little Falls, we came upon the real Little Falls! It's an exquisite waterfall in an exquisite setting. The 30-foot lacy curtain of water coasts down the sheeny shale surface, moss softening what would otherwise be sharper angles of rock. Near the bottom of the waterfall, the wall tips out slightly, creating a diminutive 1-foot free-fall curtain into the shallow pool. A fallen log provides a perfect seat to rest and enjoy the scene, accompanied by the background whisper of the falls that suggests the sprinkle of soft spring rain.

As I examined the angled fracture marks on the surface of the rock near the base of the waterfall, I was reminded of the design philosophy of master architect Frank Lloyd Wright, who was often inspired by nature to create geometric renditions of organic forms. I fancied I could see a Wrightian drawing—employing his unique grid system—of a waterfall.

We encountered no other hikers that Sunday morning, though quite a few people were enjoying the mighty Kakabeka. We suspect most visitors' experience begins and ends with the namesake waterfall, while this small, glittering jewel lies unseen in its peaceful little setting. This is a perfect example of why we invented the "Waterfall Experience" rating. Though Little Falls is not large, the setting is intimate and magical—in some ways more satisfying than the Kakabeka. You can get to know this little waterfall close up, while the Kakabeka is more like a celebrity whose picture you might snap from afar.

On the return leg of the loop, we were delighted to come upon two more really little falls. We arrived back at our car in 40 minutes.

Native Americans used the leaves of aspen trees *to treat swollen joints, headaches and burns. Parts of the bark were consumed to alleviate stomach ailments and urinary tract infections.*

Unnamed Falls

TRAILHEAD: 1.7 miles beyond Kakabeka bridge, turn right on graveled Hume Road and follow to its end, where there is a well-used grass parking turn-around. A "Danger" sign is posted by the railroad to discourage trespassing and getting hit by a train.

Follow the railroad tracks left for about 0.1 mile or four minutes, keeping an eye out for a path entering the woods on the right side of the tracks, near a dead tree. You are walking on a raised railroad bed, so should you hear a train come, you will need to get well away from the tracks. The near side of the track (in relation to parking) allows more space to walk, while the far side has a steeper bank, which would make it more difficult to scramble away. Unfortunately, that is the side with the trail, so use caution, don't dawdle, and take the near side when you return.

HIKE DIFFICULTY
Easy (except for slide down the loose rock from the railroad track bed to the path)

TRAIL QUALITY
Fair (Except for section noted above)

ROUND TRIP
0.3 mile

THE EXPERIENCE
★★ to ★★★

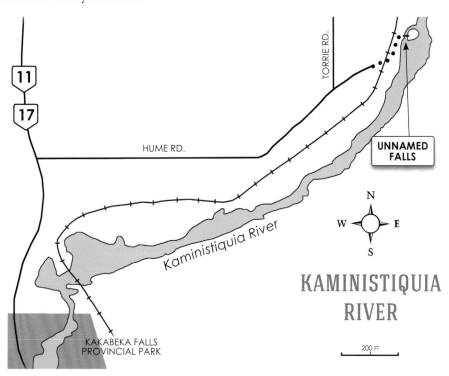

11
17

TORRIE RD.

HUME RD.

UNNAMED FALLS

Kaministiquia River

N
W ← → E
S

KAMINISTIQUIA RIVER

200 FT

KAKABEKA FALLS PROVINCIAL PARK

Getting down the railroad bank to the trail is difficult. The bank is steep and the rock loose. Whenever I encounter such conditions, I feel most safe scooting down on my derriere. Going back up always seems easier.

Once on the forest trail, hike three minutes to the rock reef through which the waterfall surges. You emerge a bit upstream. This waterfall has a unique structural configuration because the large horizontal outcrop juts out diagonally to the river's exit, where it flows into a large, lake-like section of the river.

Various perches present themselves for viewing this 8-foot waterfall, including my favorite, where the falls gush directly at you and a polished brown boulder stands its ground. The drama of the tawny bronze and black surroundings is enhanced by the charcoal-colored lichen splotching the rock.

Dog Falls

HIKE DIFFICULTY
Strenuous

TRAIL QUALITY
Poor

ROUND TRIP
2.6 miles

THE EXPERIENCE
★ ★ ★ ★ to
★ ★ ★ ★ ★
(high water)

TRAILHEAD: From the intersection of Highway 17/11 (Trans-Canadian Highway) and Highway 61 (Thunder Bay Expressway) in Thunder Bay, take 11/17 north for 3.7 miles. Turn left onto Highway 102/Dawson Road and go west for 17.4 miles. Just before the Kaministiquia River, turn right onto Silver Falls Road. At 3.6 miles the road forks. Stay to the left and proceed another 5.4 miles where the road forks, again. Stay to the left on Silver Falls Road for another 0.8 mile, following the sign for Ontario Power Hydro One Generating Plant. The road ends at a locked gate. Park to the left of the gate in the small dirt lot. Silver Falls Trail, marked by a sign, starts across the road. Definitely bring water!

The signs at the trailhead to Dog Falls are a tad schizophrenic. Although you are hiking to Dog Falls, you are hiking on Silver Falls Trail. We've seen pictures of this waterfall called by both names. But all was straightened out by the chairperson of the Thunder Bay Hiking Association. Silver Falls is the waterfall harnessed by the power plant. That waterfall is on power plant property, and access is prohibited. But the bigger and better waterfall is Dog Falls.

In addition, while one sign identifies the trail, another warns: "Danger No Entry." Well, you aren't supposed to go to Silver Falls. Signs farther on also apprise you that

Dog Falls

water levels and flow can change without warning. If this should happen, you're to head to higher ground.

This trail is maintained by the Thunder Bay Hiking Association and is generally well-marked with triangular blue signs and pink ribbons. Poor quality sections are due to rough terrain. You'll find stretches over large outcroppings where markers are sparse, but when we followed the logical paths of least resistance, we were always able to locate the next marker where the trail re-entered the woods.

Two minutes into the hike, the trail hooks up with a broad gravel road. Head right. It curves left up a hill and is flanked by wildflowers that provided us with many fluttering butterfly hiking buddies. Thirteen minutes later, almost at the top of the hill, look for the blue triangle that marks a narrow dirt trail into the woods on your right. Take this trail, and you'll soon encounter a rock outcrop with an impressive, though distant, view of the waterfalls.

A stone's throw later, if you're like me, you may be saying, "No way!" where the trail appears to drop straight down over boulders, with a knotted rope to aid your descent. Edge a bit closer and peer down before you dismiss the possibility. You'll see it's not really vertical, and along the right edges of the boulders you'll find a thin dirt path that allows you to avoid scaling down the rocks by rope. It took us five minutes to make the descent via the rope, as well as a less steep stretch sans rope.

In two minutes, head right, onto the rock outcrops, then into the woods again. Five minutes later, you'll see a sign warning of potentially changing water levels. You'll also meet a fork in the trail, with a tiny, easily missed arrow on a tree pointing left to the river. Our emergence onto the river startled a bald eagle that soared high into the azure sky.

Head back to the trail and upstream. Three minutes later you'll see masterfully stacked rocks on yet another outcrop—constructed as a sign that you are on the right track. Head right, up the outcrop, and pick up the trail marked by a blue triangle, which enters left, into the woods. In two minutes, at the next outcrop, you will arrive at the waterfalls. When we visited near the end of July, we had the additional treat of wild blueberries to snack on while we enjoyed the view.

Just upriver, you can wander about on the outcropping. You are at the top of the lowest of a series of four waterfalls—this one with about a 30-foot drop down several steps to a rock-strewn pool. You will also see, at about eye level, the two upper water-falls. We've seen a photo of this vista in spring where the whole stretch was inundated with river. As it was, the setting of the big falls, and the fractured gray and tan rock amid the pines, were spectacular. The second waterfall, to the left, is hidden behind the trees, but reveals itself as you head upriver on the outcropping.

Eight minutes later, you come to the level of the third waterfall—a 50-foot slide over smooth rocks striped in shades of rust, tan and gray—like wood grain flowing in the same direction as the water. Exploring around this waterfall and rock formation brought to mind Gooseberry Falls back in Minnesota. Head to the top of this level; the vista back toward Little Dog Lake is breathtaking, with high hills hovering at the horizon.

The fourth and top waterfall is a 20-foot slide (width and height) that flows into a fascinating square pool. Note the white stripe across the pool bottom. It continues up out of the water at the same angle, though fractured and pushed off about four feet. I had fun backing up from pool's edge to make it visually line up. Now see how the line heads toward the second drop, crosses beneath that falls too, then reappears across the stream.

Beyond the fourth, you can now see a fifth waterfall, not visible from below, about 5 feet tall with scattered potholes and other interesting erosive carvings in

In the fall, black bears *eat 15,000 calories per day to store fat for hibernation.*

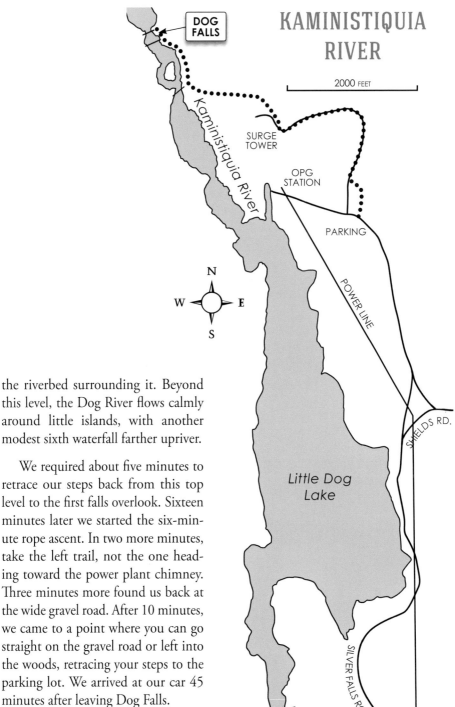

KAMINISTIQUIA RIVER

2000 FEET

the riverbed surrounding it. Beyond this level, the Dog River flows calmly around little islands, with another modest sixth waterfall farther upriver.

We required about five minutes to retrace our steps back from this top level to the first falls overlook. Sixteen minutes later we started the six-minute rope ascent. In two more minutes, take the left trail, not the one heading toward the power plant chimney. Three minutes more found us back at the wide gravel road. After 10 minutes, we came to a point where you can go straight on the gravel road or left into the woods, retracing your steps to the parking lot. We arrived at our car 45 minutes after leaving Dog Falls.

Cedar Creek Falls

CEDAR CREEK
Cedar Creek Conservation Area, Kakabeka Falls

Cedar Creek Falls

Trailhead: From the intersection of Highway 17/11 (Trans-Canadian Highway) and Highway 61 (Thunder Bay Expressway) in Thunder Bay, take Highway 11/17 west for 17.3 miles and turn left onto Highway 590, just past the town of Kakabeka Falls and after you cross over the Kaministiquia River. Go 2.6 miles and turn left onto Garbutt Road. Go 2 miles on Garbutt Road and turn left onto Broome Road. Go 1.1 miles to the Cedar Falls Conservation Area. The trail begins from the southwest corner of the parking lot.

HIKE DIFFICULTY
Easy
TRAIL QUALITY
Good
ROUND TRIP
0.6 mile
THE EXPERIENCE
★ ★ ★ to
★ ★ ★ ★

The first six minutes of the hike to Cedar Falls begins on a wide, flat, packed-dirt trail. It then descends, ascends, and in a couple more minutes you'll come to a bench, followed by 44 steps down, a slope, and 15 more steps. Another bench sits a few yards up the trail to the left if you need a rest or want a perspective on the river just downstream from this picture-perfect waterfall, which we encountered 11 minutes into our walk.

The crescent-shaped cascade ruffles white down a soft slope within a shaded grotto-like setting, with teeny ferns springing from tiny cracks. At the base of the waterfall, the river channels through a shallow, 5-foot-wide chute for about 25 feet, edging over a lip shaped like a swallow's tail before dropping a final 4 feet into a pool. The fractured black slate outcrop provides multiple spots to sit for an intimate eye-level waterfall experience. This is a superb spot to dip your feet.

Across the creek, tall spires of pine and birch climb the sky. In autumn, the foliage presents an impressionistic blend of yellow, salmon and pink. As you contemplate the peaceful scene, lulled by the shushing water, you may be further rewarded with the soft kiss of a waterfall breeze.

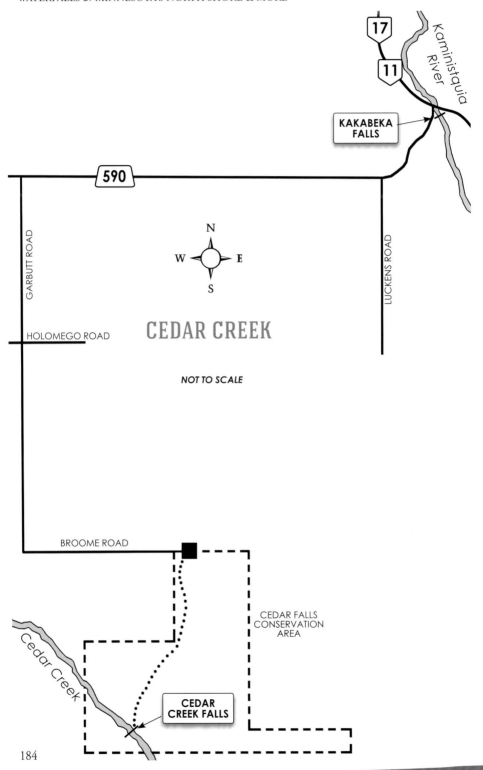

17

11

Kaministiquia River

KAKABEKA FALLS

590

GARBUTT ROAD

N
W · E
S

LUCKENS ROAD

CEDAR CREEK

HOLOMEGO ROAD

NOT TO SCALE

BROOME ROAD

CEDAR FALLS
CONSERVATION
AREA

Cedar Creek

**CEDAR
CREEK FALLS**

184

Crossing into Canada

If you're an American citizen, while you technically don't require a passport or passport card or a "trusted traveler" card to enter Canada (though you do need proof of citizenship such as a birth certificate or naturalization papers and a picture ID), you do need one to get back. So unless you're crossing to escape a zombie apocalypse and don't intend to return, you must have proper documentation for yourself and anyone else with you, including kids and dogs.

Children under 18 need their birth certificate or a copy of one, and if both parents are not along, they must have a notarized letter signed by their parents or the absent parent stating where the child is going in Canada, who is responsible, and with contact information for that parent, so border security can check, if need be. If you're the sole guardian, you are required to have papers proving that. All this is a good thing. Dogs (and cats—do yours like to hike?) at least 3 months old need proof, signed and dated by a veterinarian, that they've been vaccinated against rabies within the past year.

The border agent will ask you questions like where you're from, where you work, where you're going in Canada, for how long, and where you'll be staying. They also have the authority to search your car. Criminal convictions, including DWI's, can be reason to deny entry into Canada (even if the convicted one is not the driver). But it is ultimately up to the border agent's discretion whether to let you pass, so be on your best behavior. Think of the waterfall known as Kakabeka (a.k.a. "The Niagara of the North") on the other side—calling your name.

Mackenzie River Falls

MacKenzie River
Northeast of Thunder Bay

MacKenzie Falls

Trailhead: From the intersection of Highway 17/11 (Trans-Canadian Highway) and Highway 61 (Thunder Bay Expressway) in Thunder Bay, take Highway 17/11 northeast for 20 miles. Just after you cross over the MacKenzie River, turn left onto McKenzie Heights Road. In 0.2 mile you will intersect the new Highway 17/11. Look to your left and you'll see the highway bridge crossing over the MacKenzie River. Park on the side of McKenzie Heights Road and walk to the northwestern end of the 17/11 bridge, about 0.2 mile. Walk down beneath the bridge to the waterfall trail, which begins to your left, nearest the river, heading upstream.

HIKE DIFFICULTY
Easy (though if there's road construction, it requires scrambling down and up loose rock from the trailhead)

TRAIL QUALITY
Fair

ROUND TRIP
0.6 mile from bridge, but 1 mile from McKenzie Heights Road where we parked

THE EXPERIENCE
★★★ to
★★★★

Depending upon the status of the bridge construction, the beginning of this path may abut vinyl sheeting erected to control erosion into the river, but even so, the trail is easy to find. Upholstered in pine needles and woven with roots from ancient cedars, the path walks you upstream, at river level, through boreal surroundings. It also passes the loveliest blanket of club moss we've encountered. Though echoing the appearance of the evergreens that tower above them, these interesting, prehistoric ground plants are miniatures.

Shortly into your stroll, you must cross a small stream that parallels the river, then pick up the path on the other side. In a couple of minutes, you'll see the beginnings of gorge walls as the trail meanders back into the woods. Three minutes later, and about 15 minutes from starting out at the trailhead, you'll negotiate a patch of smooth rocks and boulders under a clump of large cedar. Keep following the water's edge for about 30 more feet to emerge onto a rock outcropping. You'll hear MacKenzie

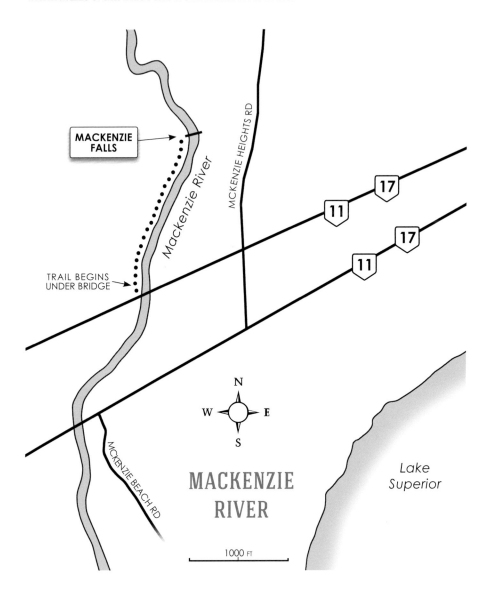

Falls—it's loud—though not yet see it. Note where someone has painted the white outline of a figure on the rock outcrop beneath your feet, as well as an arrow that points toward the waterfall viewpoint and the boulder you wind around to access the foot of the falls.

MacKenzie Falls is enclosed between high black walls through which it dives about 20 feet into a pool, then narrows to a 6-foot flume into another pool with a rock bottom and a scattering of large boulders. This waterfall is of the free-fall variety—descending in a curtain away from the rock rather than along it, though smaller trickles scramble down the wall to the right of the main falls. The crash of the waterfall into the pool creates a picturesque and refreshing mist. Sitting at the base of the falls, see if you can find the small pothole beneath the water's surface. It's just right for a barefooted heel to rest nicely.

Though we hated to leave this entrancing area, other waterfalls called, as did the rocks veined with amethyst crystals that we'd spotted beneath the highway bridge just before the trailhead. Too bad we weren't parked closer, and the day wasn't so darned hot, or we'd have carried back more treasure.

The largest amethyst mine *in North America is located in Thunder Bay.*

Lower Falls in the Wolf River

UPPER WOLF RIVER

Dorion

Lower Falls

Trailhead: From the intersection of Highway 17/11 (Trans-Canadian Highway) and Highway 61 (Thunder Bay Expressway) in Thunder Bay, take Highway 17/11 northeast for 48.5 miles. Turn left onto Fish Hatchery Road and proceed 1.1 miles. Take the 90-degree right turn and continue on Fish Hatchery Road for another 1.4 miles at which point you will again take another 90-degree turn to the right. In 1 mile, the road will take a 90-degree left to a gated gravel road, marked by a "No vehicles" sign, heading off to your right. Park here. Go through the gate on the dirt and gravel road, which heads downhill. Just before the bottom, about five minutes into the hike, take the overgrown road to the left. Continue three minutes to the river, where the road ends.

HIKE DIFFICULTY
Strenuous
TRAIL QUALITY
Good to Poor
ROUND TRIP
0.9 miles
THE EXPERIENCE
★ ★ ★ ★

At water's edge, you'll see a narrow trail going right, into the woods. You must push through the pine branches, though the path beneath your feet is well-trod and clear to see. In a minute, you'll encounter a small clearing where you can see the upper portion of the falls. Don't stop here. Re-enter the pines and head downriver for a few yards, then climb down a large rock. In a couple more yards, you'll spy a yellow knotted rope to your left, tied to a tree. This is your way to river level below the falls. It's not as hard as it looks, and I even found it fun. It took two minutes to scramble down.

Lower Falls, at about 25 feet high, has the wow! factor—a three-quarter view of white water gushing around a huge spear-head-shaped rock, the right side in higher water than the left. Gigantic boulders below the promontory provide another opportunity for the water to churn before it calms, though you can see some more smaller falls downriver.

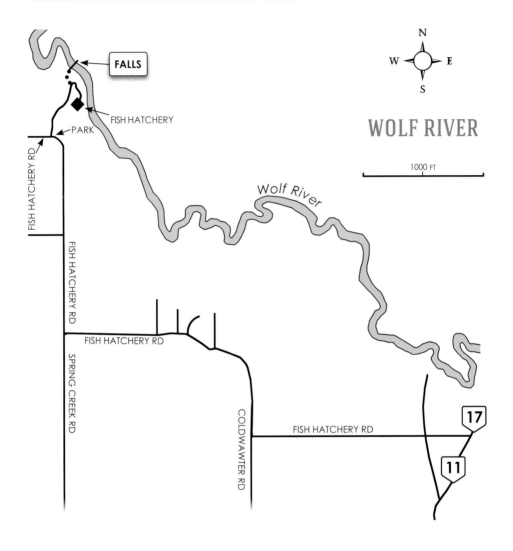

FALLS

FISH HATCHERY

PARK

FISH HATCHERY RD

FISH HATCHERY RD

FISH HATCHERY RD

SPRING CREEK RD

COLDWAWTER RD

FISH HATCHERY RD

Wolf River

N
W E
S

WOLF RIVER

1000 FT

17

11

If you want to get closer to the maelstrom, make your way carefully up the rocks to the left of the falls. Talk about a waterfall experience—we didn't want to leave! The rope climb up was a little tricky, but six minutes later, we were back on the gravel uphill road, which is just steep enough to make your thighs burn and heart pump. Nine minutes more, and we were back to our car.

Moose *are herbivores and eat 50-60 pounds of plants per day, though they have no upper front teeth They can run as fast as 35 miles-per-hour and can swim six miles-per-hour for two hours.*

Wisconsin Waterfalls

DULUTH, MN

35

Lake Superior

SUPERIOR, WI

2

35

Black R.

Amnicon R.

53

Though I was born in Racine, Wisconsin and lived my first twenty-some years there, I didn't see my first Wisconsin waterfall (not counting the 20-foot-tall spill of Root River over Horlick Dam) until my teens—Amnicon Falls in Amnicon Falls State Park. My best friend, Martha Keller (we both loved horses and hated boys) invited me to travel with her family to camp at Trails End campground on the Gunflint Trail in Minnesota—a long trip from the southeast corner of Wisconsin—and we stopped at Amnicon on the way. I recall Paul McCartney's Uncle Albert/Admiral Halsey playing repeatedly on the radio during the drive. It was 1971.

In addition to seeing my first Wisconsin waterfall on that trip, I saw my first Minnesota waterfall—Gooseberry Falls—and got my first taste of the North Shore and its boreal forests. First time I camped (not counting Girl Scout camp with the raised wooden-floored tents), first time I saw reindeer lichen (it blew my mind we were so far north that reindeer food actually grew here), first time I slept outside in the company of bears (her dad told us one strolled by our tent in the night), first time I saw the northern lights. It strikes me now what a pivotal trip that was in planting the seeds for my love of both waterfalls and Minnesota's North Shore. Thank you, Martha.

The Wisconsin waterfalls Gary and I visited for this edition of the book have a different lay-out than those of the North Shore. They also live in rivers that flow into Lake Superior, formed 12,000 years ago during the big glacial melt

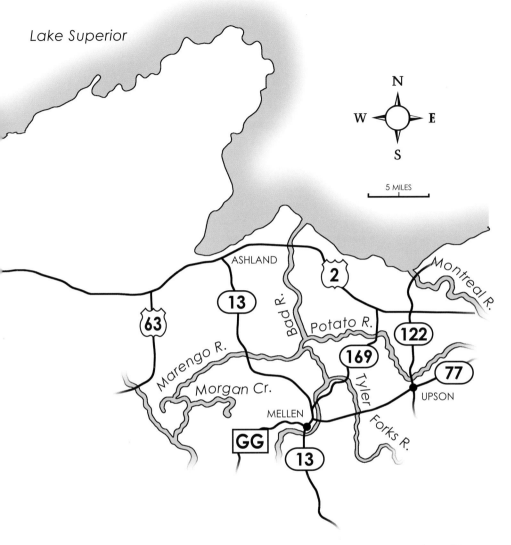

that created the Great Lakes. But unlike Minnesota's dense series of long, steep river canyons so near the lake, the grade is more gradual along the Wisconsin side, with the exception of Superior Falls in Lake Superior County Park.

Must-sees include Pattison State Park, only 13 miles south of Superior, Wisconsin. This is home to Wisconsin's highest waterfall, Big Manitou Falls, and 4-star Little Manitou Falls, which is in no way "Little." Also Amnicon Falls State Park, just 14 miles from Superior, makes for a lovely waterfall hike on a piney river island. Copper Falls State Park is a bit more of a trek at 88 miles, but its beautiful 4-star Dough Boys Trail waterfall loop is worth it. And…well, read on for yourself. You decide!

Big Manitou Falls

BLACK RIVER
Pattison State Park

Big Manitou Falls

Trailhead: From the intersection of Highways 2 and 35 in Superior, Wis., take Highway 35 (Tower Avenue) south 13.1 miles. Just after crossing the Black River, turn right onto East County Road B then into a small parking lot on your left. From the east end of the parking lot, walk back across County Road B towards the river. A sign directs you to overlooks of Big Manitou Falls, named "Gitchi Manitou" by Native Americans.

Big Manitou Falls, at 165 feet, is the tallest waterfall in Wisconsin, comparable to the High Falls of the Pigeon River in Minnesota. The big difference is the opportunity to experience this waterfall close up.

HIKE DIFFICULTY
Easy and wheelchair accessible to first overlook

TRAIL QUALITY
Good to first overlook

ROUND TRIP
0.1 mile

THE EXPERIENCE
★ ★ ★ ★ ★

The trail is well-paved and wheelchair accessible, with even the amenity of an outhouse. When we viewed this waterfall, my husband put it eloquently, "Wow, that is one big frickin' waterfall!"

The torrent zigzags over rocks into a relatively small pothole. Looking across the waterfall, you see dark rust-colored rock adorned with patches of orange lichen and evergreen trees, as well as the overlook on the other side of the falls.

For two more overlooks (neither as impressive as the first), follow the paved trail to the left (hole-pitted and not wheelchair accessible) steeply down through maple and oak to a rough wooden overlook. Here you get a head-on view of the waterfall. Breathe in the piney scent. A third overlook provides another view. This is an easy hike except for a short steep section. We made it back to our car in about seven minutes.

Lake Superior *is the largest fresh water lake in the world. One inch of surface water is equal to 533 billion gallons.*

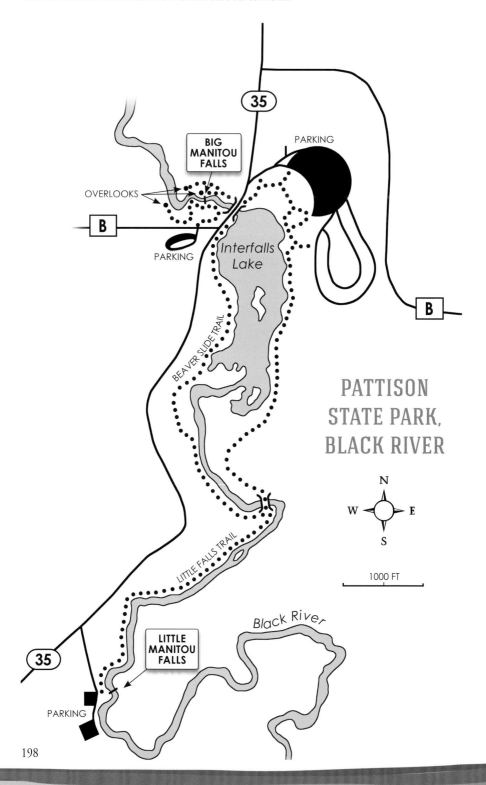

35

PARKING

BIG MANITOU FALLS

OVERLOOKS

B

PARKING

Interfalls Lake

B

BEAVER SLIDE TRAIL

PATTISON STATE PARK, BLACK RIVER

N
W E
S

1000 FT

LITTLE FALLS TRAIL

Black River

35

LITTLE MANITOU FALLS

PARKING

For other perspectives of Big Manitou Falls, take County Road B back to 35, and head left over the bridge. In about 100 feet, a trail—part paved, part pressed gravel—goes left along the other side of the river to other viewing platforms.

Water pours out of the lake, over a dam and down rocks. Continue ahead a short ways, up 20 steps to the viewing platform, which also features an informational plaque. Continue down another 25 steps to another platform and another "Wow!" view. You're at the brink of the waterfall powerfully plunging down that middle section you saw from below.

Big Manitou Falls

But there's yet another overlook, which you can see from this one, and that you know is going to be cool. Go back up the wide, shallow railroad-tie steps. Then descend down seven steep, narrow cement steps onto a wooden viewing platform for a spectacular view. The waterfall is on your left, narrow yet packing a wallop, producing loads of suds and foam—perhaps more than we've seen at any other waterfall along the shore. Look to your right for an ethereal view of the panoramic green canyon, running for miles off into the distance.

The name "Big Manitou Falls" comes from Native Americans who said they could hear the voice of the Great Spirit in the roaring water, calling it "Gitche Manitou." *Two rare species have been found in the gorge —Oregon Woodsia and the Mystery Vertigo land snail.*

Little Manitou Falls

HIKE DIFFICULTY
Easy

TRAIL QUALITY
Good

ROUND TRIP
0.1 mile

THE EXPERIENCE
★ ★ ★ ★

TRAILHEAD: Little Manitou Falls is a few miles upstream from Big Manitou Falls. From the Big Manitou parking lot, head right on East County Road B to Highway 35. Turn right on 35 and go south 0.9 miles. A sign directs you to turn left (east) to Little Manitou Falls. After turning, proceed 500 feet to park on your right. The clearly marked trailhead directs you across the road.

You can hear the call of Little Manitou Falls from the parking lot. A crushed-granite path brings you to a wooden bridge, then across a park road. The mixed deciduous and pine woods preside above a forest floor abundant with ferns, false lily of the valley and blue bead lily.

The Little Manitou defies its name. Wow again! There is no formal overlook, just a gravel clearing with no guard rail. This waterfall is more than 30 feet tall, and the rock looks blacker and less worn than that of the Big Manitou. A bench to the right provides a relaxing spot to view the splendor, while feeling the cool breath of the falls against your face.

The Little Manitou is satisfyingly close—like its big brother. You can also venture farther to the right to large rock steps and a path beyond that to water level.

Wisconsin has a small but growing herd of wild elk *(approximately 180) living in the Clam Lake area of Ashland County. They were reintroduced by the University of Wisconsin-Stevens Point in 1995.*

Little Manitou Falls

Upper Amnicon Falls

AMNICON RIVER
Amnicon Falls State Park

Upper and Lower Amnicon Falls, The Snake Pit

Trailhead: From the intersection of Highways 2 and 35 in Superior, Wis., head 1.7 miles east on Highway 2 (Belknap Street). Turn right on East Second Street, also called Highway 2/53, and go southeast 11.3 miles. Stay to the left on Highway 2 where 2 and 53 fork and drive one more mile. Turn left onto County Road U for 0.3 mile. Turn left into the park on Park Road for 0.1 mile, then turn right following the road to a large parking lot. At the northwest end, a sign reads, "Lower Falls."

HIKE DIFFICULTY
Easy
TRAIL QUALITY
Good
ROUND TRIP
0.25 mile
THE EXPERIENCE
★★ to ★★★★

A paved trail leads to a bridge from which you can gaze upstream to Upper Falls. The water flowed in a torrent on the August day we visited. The broad, 20-foot waterfall flows around two huge boulders hunched in the middle of the river. White pines cling to rock edges. And all of this can be viewed from the unique shelter of a quaint covered bridge.

Cross the bridge to the island around which the Amnicon River flows. The 0.25 mile trail gives you access to the three main waterfalls: another perspective on the Upper, as well as the Lower and The Snake Pit. It also leads you to other smaller waterfalls and pools, and an additional 0.5 mile of trails.

Lower Amnicon Falls, about 15 feet high, flows below the bridge. Geologically, this is a particularly interesting stretch of river. It resembles a topo map, the scouring power of the river vividly illustrated by its undercutting of multiple rock layers. Head upriver to where benches beckon you to contemplate nature's beauty and the strength of her rivers.

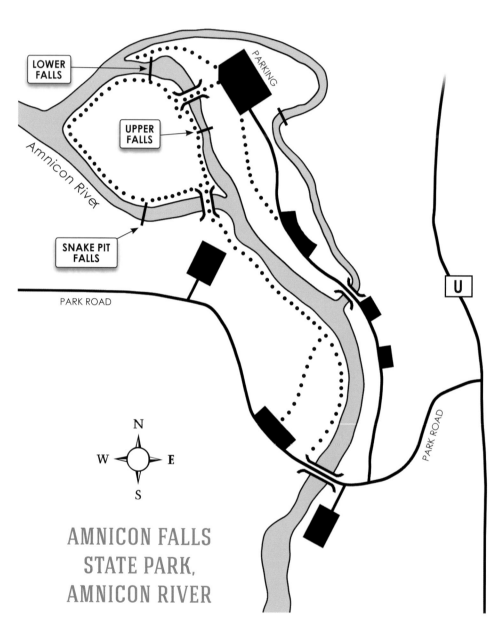

LOWER
FALLS

PARKING

UPPER
FALLS

Amnicon River

SNAKE PIT
FALLS

PARK ROAD

U

PARK ROAD

N
W · E
S

AMNICON FALLS
STATE PARK,
AMNICON RIVER

1000 FT

Flow here fluctuates. We noted much more water on a previous visit, even though it certainly wasn't lacking this day. Majestic pines along the river create a cathedral-like air. Picnic tables in scattered piney clearings throughout this river island are heavenly spots to enjoy a snack, as the pounding of the riotous river and pine perfume permeate your senses.

Moving farther upriver, you'll see water on both sides of you as you approach the headland around which the river splits. An overlook about 100 yards up from the bridge features rapids writhing among red rocks. A last little bridge provides a lovely spot to linger and be mesmerized by swirling water and beautiful views.

Follow the fork of the river that edges along the far side of the island, making your way over the blan-

Lower Falls

ket of pine needles. Enjoy multiple little waterfalls as you wander the perimeter of the island. You'll encounter the remnants of a foot bridge that looks like a pair of mammoth wheels, which was likely washed away by spring floods. During certain times of the year, you'll see wild rosebushes blooming just below the "wheels." You will recognize "The Snake Pit" when you come upon it. The river is very wide here, and the 25-foot waterfall strikes down hard into its large "pit," then slithers quickly away through high, dark canyon walls where ferns cling on for dear life.

Morgan Creek Falls

MORGAN CREEK
Chequamegon–Nicolet National Forest

Morgan Falls

TRAILHEAD: From the intersection of Highways 2 and 35 in Superior, Wis., head east on Highway 2 (Belknap St) for 1.7 miles. Turn right onto Highway 53 South/East Second Street and continue for 11.3 miles. Stay left on Highway 2 East when 2 and 53 split, then continue for 42.9 miles. Turn right onto Highway 63 South. Go 8.8 miles and turn left onto County Highway E. Proceed 6 miles. Turn right at Our Savior Lutheran Church onto County Line Road (also called Ashland/Bayfield Road or Four Corners Store Road) and continue 4.4 miles. The parking area for both Morgan Falls and St. Peter's Dome trails is on your left.

HIKE DIFFICULTY	Easy
TRAIL QUALITY	Good
ROUND TRIP	1.2 miles
THE EXPERIENCE	★★★ to ★★★★

We embarked upon Morgan Falls trail just as a gentle, drifting mist began falling. But we welcomed the sudden cloud cover and coolness on such a hot Fourth of July day. The crushed gravel trail soon transitioned to a flat wooden bridge, which forded a small creek that meandered through ferns, birch and maple. Soon after, we encountered a second bridge framed by maidenhair fern and blue bead lily. Moss abounded, upholstering rocks and tree trunks in vivid green. Jack-in-the-pulpit, Solomon's seal, and star flower added to the luxurious mix. Soon we crossed another trickle of a stream.

Fifteen minutes into our hike, we came upon a bigger stream, which we traversed on yet another flat wooden bridge. The path took a sharp right, past a beaver pond, and rose slightly. Only two minutes past that stream, a sign read: "Left to St. Peter's Dome, Right to Morgan Falls." More bridges kept us above what was now only a trickle of a creek, but soon we descended again to water level and our destination—Morgan Creek Falls.

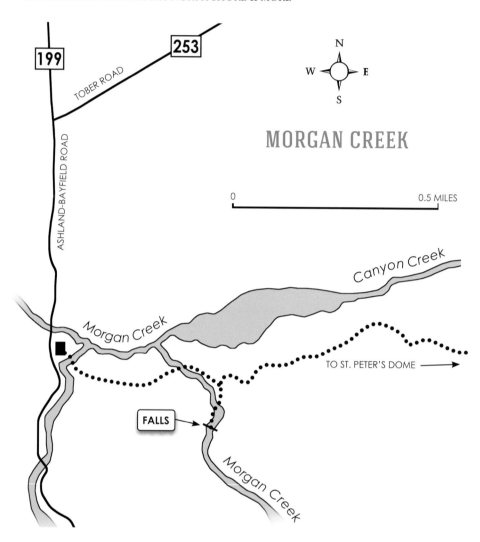

Morgan Creek Falls sits like a gem in a small but exquisite setting. Like Hidden Falls on the Split Rock River, it's intimate, as Mother Earth hugs these precious places protectively to her breast. This waterfall is one of the tallest in the state, listed variously at 70 to 100 feet. It's a thin ribbon of water, descending back and forth through a V-shaped divot in the cracked rock face. The top is not visible from the bottom, much like Caribou Falls in Minnesota, so if reported heights are accurate, we may be viewing only about half of its true height from the base.

St. Peter's Dome, *near Morgan Falls, is known locally as "Old Baldy" and stands tall at 1565 feet. From its top, on a clear day you can see the Cheguamegon Bay of Lake Superior and the Apostle islands 20 miles away.*

Copper Fallls

TYLER FORKS & BAD RIVER
Copper Falls State Park

Copper Falls, Brownstone Falls, Tyler Forks Cascades

Trailhead: Head east on Hwy 2 E. for 1.7 mi. Turn right onto U.S. 53 E Second Street and continue 11.3 miles. Stay left on Hwy. 2 when it splits with Hwy 53. Continue 43 miles. Turn right onto U.S. 63 S. and go 2.6 mi. Turn left onto WI 118E and go 6.8 mi. Turn left onto WI 112 S. and go 7.4 mi. Turn right onto WI 13 S and go 13 Mi. Turn left onto WI 169 N. Go 1.7 Mi. to Copper Falls Road. Turn Left and go 1.5 miles and then another slight left for 500 feet to the parking area. From the parking lot, walk past the log concession building. You will see a sign for "The Doughboys' Trail." Please note that dogs are not allowed on this trail.

HIKE DIFFICULTY
Easy to Strenuous, depending upon how far you go. Wheelchair accessible to Copper Falls

TRAIL QUALITY
Good

ROUND TRIP
1.7 miles on Doughboys' Trail

THE EXPERIENCE
★★★★

See three major waterfalls along "Doughboys' Trail" loop as it wends its way beneath hemlock and pine. We proceeded counter-clockwise, edging the east side of the Bad River. Shortly, you will climb 26 steps to a beautiful Civilian Conservation Corps-constructed overlook of 29-foot Copper Falls. The river divides around a large outcropping with the right side dropping dramatically over several steps before joining the left in a large pool to continue through the gorge. Copper Falls, by itself, earns three stars. It is an impressive waterfall but lacks a good, close view.

A short, pleasant stroll brings you to another overlook—this one of 30-foot Brownstone Falls, where the Tyler Forks tributary meets up with the Bad River. This

---

Just a few thousand years ago, Lake Superior held so much water, it was high enough to leave old beach lines *in Copper Falls State Park.*

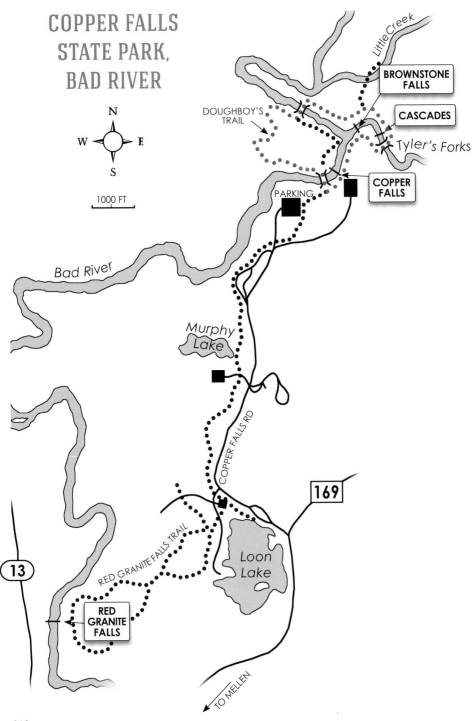

COPPER FALLS STATE PARK, BAD RIVER

Little Creek

BROWNSTONE FALLS

DOUGHBOY'S TRAIL

CASCADES

Tyler's Forks

N
W · E
S

PARKING

COPPER FALLS

1000 FT

Bad River

Murphy Lake

COPPER FALLS RD

169

13

RED GRANITE FALLS TRAIL

Loon Lake

RED GRANITE FALLS

TO MELLEN

waterfall was named after the richly colored, high rock canyon—formed by ancient red lava flows—through which it plunges. An informational sign also references the U-shaped overflow channel formed during glacial melt. It still serves its purpose during floods, directing water into the river gorge.

Leaving Brownstone Falls overlook, you descend seven steps and continue on the trail along the fence line. In a few moments, you'll see and hear a nice series of cascades, and soon after, even more. Five minutes after leaving the Brownstone Falls overlook, a bridge crosses the Tyler Forks river. Heading left, downriver, you will shortly come to a lovely overlook of the Tyler Forks Cascades below. We also encountered some strange, stiff grass to the right of the trail that felt and looked like curly wire.

Fifteen steps head down to another cascade overlook where the water meets you head-on, with the footbridge you just crossed visible in the distance. For us, this was the most impressive waterfall view in the park. These cascades are a series of roiling falls, a scene of the elemental battle between rock and water. Water flows down multiple levels and though the drops are not very big, taken as a whole, it is highly picturesque.

Climbing back up from the overlook is challenging, but before too long the trail levels out and begins to descend. Soon you'll happen upon an old moss-covered, two-sided, roofed bench. A couple minutes later, 37 steps descend to a river overlook, then 87 more steps down to a bridge. Cross the bridge over the Bad River, and go left, upriver. The trail will climb over four flights of steps, 100 in all, to another overlook—sheesh!—of Devil's Gate, a conglomerate rock outcropping. Fortunately, benches are placed along the way. Nevertheless, this changed our rating of the hike from easy to strenuous. What do you think? We were happy to get back to shade and drinks at the concession area, but also happy we'd had the chance to hike this great waterfall trail.

(Another waterfall, Red Granite Falls, is accessible via a loop in the south end of the park. We've seen pictures, and weren't impressed enough to tackle it on that hot day. It looks more like a series of cascades than a waterfall. If you are more compulsive than we are, though, check it out and let us know!)

The 7000-member Bad River Band is one of six Ojibwe bands in Wisconsin. Traveling from the east coast of the St. Lawrence River area, legend tells of a search for a place where food grew in the water (wild rice). Odanah (meaning "village") was originally located at the confluence of the Bad and White Rivers. The area was known as "Gete Gititaaning," *meaning "the old garden." This area is rich in topsoil due to river flooding and is where the native people would plant their gardens and return to harvest them in the fall.*

Upper Potato Falls

POTATO RIVER
Southwest of Gurney

Upper Potato Falls

Trailhead: From the intersection of Highway 2 (Belknap Street) and Highway 35 (Tower Avenue) in Superior, Wisconsin, head east on Highway 2 East for 1.7 miles. Turn right onto Highway 53 South/East Second Street and continue for 11.3 miles. Where Highways 2 and 53 split, stay left on Highway 2 East and proceed 73.2 miles. Turn right onto State Highway 169 South (there will be a gas station on your left) and go 2.8 miles. Just past the tiny town of Gurney, turn right onto Falls Road for 1 mile. The road makes a 90-degree turn to the left. Go another 0.5 mile to a parking area. The trails to Potato River Falls begin from the parking area.

HIKE DIFFICULTY	Moderate
TRAIL QUALITY	Fair
ROUND TRIP	0.3 mile
THE EXPERIENCE	★★★ to ★★★★

Follow the trail from the southeast end of the parking area. It soon turns into a stretch of 130 steps that lead you to an observation deck providing a broad view of the Upper Falls.

Upper Falls is a magnificent composition—a four-level cascade over shardy black rock flanked by majestic greenery. The series begins tentatively, then builds as it flows downriver to a wide, lacy level, then drops about 20 feet. The river wraps both sides around a huge lichen-encrusted outcrop, the left side forming a voluminous V, then scampers down more steps, joining to fall another 30 feet into a small pool. Pines cling to the right of the waterfall on rock splattered in pale green lichen. Then the water plunges another 20 feet.

The observation deck is poised just above the fourth drop, making it difficult to see below. Beneath that platform is another undeveloped overlook with no rail, accessible down a tiny path requiring you to brace your feet against rocks. From there you can see the fourth cascade, narrower than the three previous. At the bottom, the flow pauses, then continues 200 feet downriver to the Lower Falls.

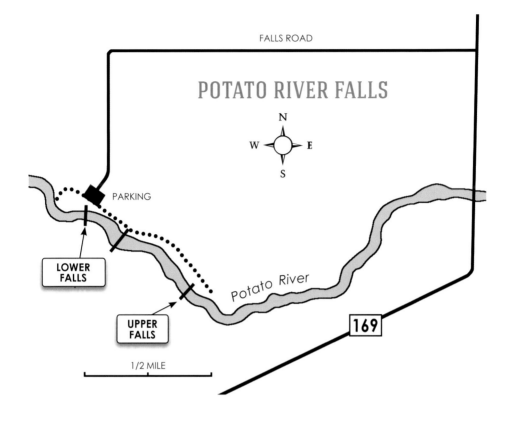

From this undeveloped overlook, it's possible, though not advisable, to make your way to river level, if you're nimble and have good shoes. Retrace your way right and take the little dirt trail where it descends to water's edge. It's very rough going, with only roots as steps, and rocks and trees to cling to, so don't lose your footing. Or maybe just avoid this part altogether...

At river level, the rocks are large and square. From a spit of land close to the base of this waterfall, note alternating stripes of milk chocolate and dark chocolate browns melting from one side of the river, flowing beneath the water, emerging on the other side.

If you continue downstream a few yards, you come to the brink of the bottom-most part of the waterfall. Gaze downstream for a fascinating geological creation that looks as though someone wielding a wide brush swept one mighty reddish paint stroke down the rock.

Heading back up is strenuous, even before you encounter all those steps again. We had to rest.

Lower Potato Falls

An observation deck immediately off the southwest end of the parking area offers a high view of the Lower Falls. For a closer look, go to the northwest side of the parking area and take the packed dirt foot path marked with a brown sign that reads, "Trail to river—Lower Falls." It leads you down a slight decline through conifer trees and yew, the waterfall audible the entire time. Only one minute from the parking lot, you'll emerge onto a point of land with a perilous descending side-path. Instead, continue straight along the much-used sandy path. Two minutes later, 31 wooden steps (*sans* railings) head down to a little square observation deck with views of Lower Potato River Falls. The view isn't very satisfying, though, because vegetation partially blocks the main part of the falls. What you do see clearly is the first and smaller drop. A full view of the waterfall would be rather impressive. After the initial 10-foot drop, it falls again about 30 feet in a lacy sheet over an almost vertical face of rock 60 feet wide.

HIKE DIFFICULTY
Moderate
TRAIL QUALITY
Fair
ROUND TRIP
<0.1 mile
THE EXPERIENCE
★ ★

Marinette County *markets itself as the "Waterfall Capitol of Wisconsin," but Iron County is tops with the most falls, including five of the ten tallest.*

Foster Falls

HIKE DIFFICULTY
Easy

TRAIL QUALITY
Fair

ROUND TRIP
<0.1 mile

THE EXPERIENCE
★★ to ★★★

Trailhead: From the intersection of U.S. Highway 2 (Belknap Street) and Highway 35 (Tower Avenue) in Superior, Wis., head east on Highway 2 for 1.7 miles and turn right onto U.S. Highway 53 South/East Second Street. Continue for 11.3 miles, and when Highway 53 and Highway 2 split, stay left on U.S. Highway 2 East. Continue for 77.8 miles. Turn right onto 122 South/Hoyt Road and proceed for 4.8 miles. Turn right onto Sullivan Road and go another 2.9 miles. The road ends where the Potato River has washed out a bridge. About 100 yards before the river, a dirt road heads to your right or north. Take it for about 200 yards to the end and park. It is just a few steps down to the falls.

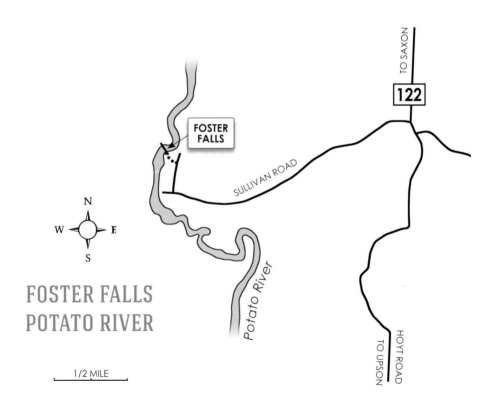

FOSTER FALLS
POTATO RIVER

1/2 MILE

As soon as you leave your car, you can hear Foster Falls calling. Follow the dirt path to the waterfall. We continued downstream from where the path emerged at the river, where we had a better view, though the path petered out. From this pleasant spot, you see the lower portion of 25-foot Foster Falls as it slides over the slanted, polished rock face into a tranquil pool. Looking right, the pool narrows to become a shallow stream flowing through deep woods.

Foster Falls

The male turkey *begins to gobble and strut as part of the breeding courtship around April or May, although some displays begin as early as January. Generally the roosting males will gobble in the roost tree before flying down to display on the ground just after sunrise.*

Superior Falls

MONTREAL RIVER
Lake Superior County Park

Superior Falls

Trailhead: From the intersection of U.S. Highway 2 East (Belknap Street) and Highway 35 (Tower Avenue) in Superior, Wis., head east on Highway 2 for 1.7 miles and turn right onto U.S. Highway 53 South/ East Second Street. Continue for 11.3 miles. When Highway 2 and Highway 53 split, stay left on U.S. Highway 2 East. Continue for 77.8 miles. Turn left onto 122 North/ Hoyt Road and proceed for 4.2 miles. You will cross over the Montreal River into Michigan. Continue onto County Highway 505/Lake Superior Road for 0.4 mile. Turn left. It is a short drive to the power station and then you will see a sign that says "Waterfall." Park where the road ends to the right of the power station. Excel Energy operates the Superior Falls Hydro plant and keeps the area open to the public.

HIKE DIFFICULTY
Moderate
TRAIL QUALITY
Good
ROUND TRIP
0.6 mile
THE EXPERIENCE
★★★ to ★★★★

Size estimates of this waterfall vary from 90 to 110 feet. It is made up of three large drops. To view the lower and largest part of the waterfall from below, take the paved trail that leaves the parking area to the right of the substation. A sign marks the beginning of this trail: "Montreal River Scenic Overlook Access Trail." It descends steeply down to Lake Superior. At the bottom of the grade, just before the beach, a trail heads off to the left toward the power plant, 100 yards away. Follow this path. When you get to the power house, go behind it and continue upriver another 50 yards. You will find yourself at the bottom of falls. This is an impressive, broad waterfall, about 65 feet in height.

Blueberries *have been found to help protect against cancer, improve brain functioning, slow aging, prevent heart attacks and strokes, decrease belly fat, and improve eyesight.*

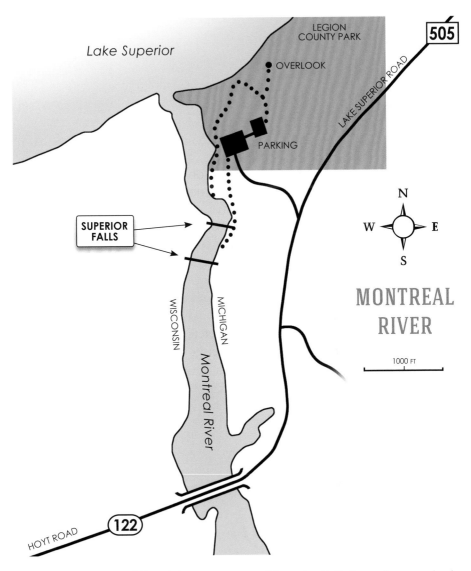

To view this waterfall and the upper parts of Superior Falls from above, go back on the road from the parking lot to the fenced-in substation. To the left of this, follow the well-trod path upstream along the edge of the river canyon. A chain link fence has been erected to keep you from plummeting over the edge. You will be able to catch sight of the two upper drops of the waterfall as you proceed. When the fence ends, make your way down closer to the upper falls. The path is not easy or obvious and not one for small children. When you come to the 25-foot upper falls, you'll see a large sign warning that the water level can change dramatically when the dam just above the falls is opened.

Saxon Falls

TRAILHEAD: From the intersection of U.S. Highway 2 East (Belknap Street) and Highway 35 (Tower Avenue) in Superior, Wis, head east on Highway 2 for 1.7 miles and turn right onto U.S. Highway 53 South/East Second Street. Continue for 11.3 miles. When Highway 2 and Highway 53 split, stay left on U.S. Highway 2 East. Continue for 77.8 miles. Turn left onto 122 North and proceed for 2.1 miles. Turn right onto West County Road B. Go 1.7 miles. Turn left onto Saxon Falls Road and go 0.2 mile, then turn right and follow this 0.7 mile to the end of the road, where you can park.

HIKE DIFFICULTY
Easy
TRAIL QUALITY
Good
ROUND TRIP
0.5 mile
THE EXPERIENCE
★★ to ★★★

A dirt road heads down hill to the left. Follow this to a large black pipe going over the river. Your hike to the waterfall begins by walking on the metal grate (with rails) above the pipe for about 100 yards to a concrete platform. Turn left. The walkway will soon end at a well-worn dirt and pine needle path that winds through ferns and evergreen trees.

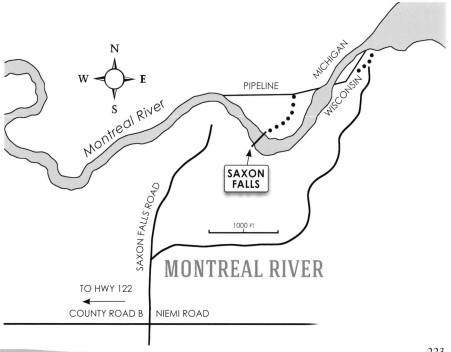

Saxon Falls

When you emerge three minutes later, you'll hear the sound of the water. The path is just above the river. You're at the top of Saxon Falls. The view isn't spectacular—mainly just the hole into which the water falls. Downstream you can see a white building and footbridge. Make your way down the rocks to the lacy white cascade. The coniferous canyon is a geological masterpiece, heavily sculpted with rock mounds and potholes.

Interstate Falls

TRAILHEAD: From the intersection of U.S. Highway 2 East (Belknap Street) and Highway 35 (Tower Avenue) in Superior, Wis., head east on Highway 2 for 1.7 miles and turn right onto U.S. Highway 53 South/East Second Street. Continue for 11.3 miles. When Highway 2 and Highway 53 split, stay left on U.S. Highway 2 East. Continue for 88.3 miles. Just before Highway 2 intersects Highway 51, turn left onto a gravel road (West Center Drive). Watch carefully because West Center Drive may be unmarked but there should be a small, white, arrow-shaped sign that says "Peterson Falls." Continue on West Center Drive. In 0.2 mile, it will turn right, but you will continue straight for about another 0.1 mile. You will pass another turn to the right that goes into an old sand pit. Stay left for a short distance, then the road makes a turn to the right. When you go around this corner, you can park on your right at a dirt turn-off. Across the road, to your left, there should be a trail heading north to the falls.

HIKE DIFFICULTY
Easy (unless you scale down to the falls)

TRAIL QUALITY
Fair

ROUND TRIP
0.6 mile

THE EXPERIENCE
★★ to ★★★

Interstate Falls

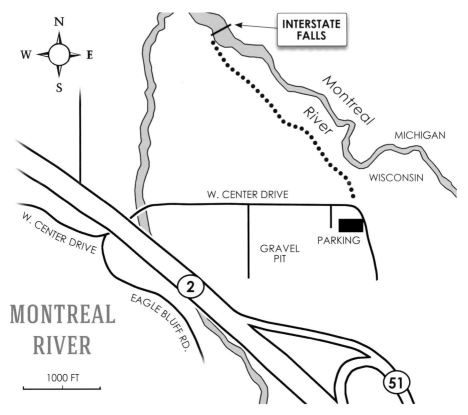

A good deal of confusing information exists regarding "Interstate Falls," "Peterson Falls," and "Montreal Falls." We think we straightened it out. The U.S. Geological Survey identified two distinct waterfalls here: Interstate and Peterson. Peterson is a cascade about a half-mile upriver from Interstate Falls, on private land owned by the Petersons. We are directing you to Interstate Falls, which also is known as Montreal Falls. This trail also passes through private property, but public access has been allowed for many years. As of this writing, the land is for sale, however, so we can't guarantee this will be true indefinitely. But if you're in the area already, this is an enjoyable and easy hike, and it's worth checking out.

Soon the trail forks to the right. Skip that fork and continue straight ahead. About 10 minutes into the hike—you can't miss it—you will emerge at the top of Interstate Falls. If you want, it is possible to scale your way down the 10 feet to the bottom, using tree roots and rocks as steps. This is the only part of the hike that's difficult. I would not recommend it for children. This is a decent waterfall, about 15 to 20 feet, as broad as it is high. The water hits a huge rock projection on the lower right side and falls into a small pool, allowing you to get close—about 30 feet from the waterfall.